BRITAIN'S
LAST INVASION
Fishguard 1797

Beth,

Dydd pen blwydd hapus
2015

from the author

Teddy x

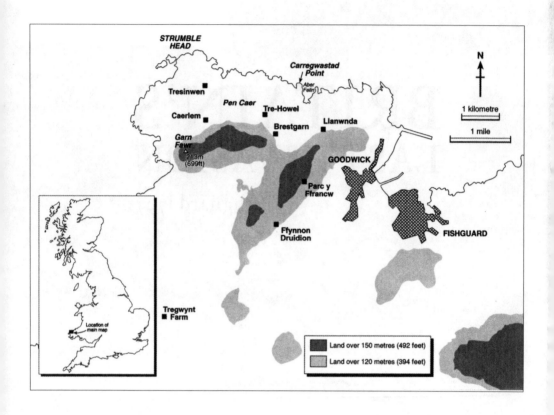

STRUMBLE
HEAD

Carregwastad
Point

Aber
Felin

Tresinwen

Pen Caer

Tre-Howel

Caerlem

Brestgarn

Llanwnda

Garn
Fawr
213m
(699ft)

GOODWICK

Parc y
Ffrancw

Ffynnon
Druidion

FISHGUARD

Location of
main map

Tregwynt
Farm

N

1 kilometre

1 mile

Land over 150 metres (492 feet)

Land over 120 metres (394 feet)

BRITAIN'S
LAST INVASION

Fishguard 1797

J.E. THOMAS

TEMPUS

Frontispiece: Map showing key places mentioned in the text. (Drawn by Chris Lewis.)

Cover illustration: Contemporary painting of the French landing at Carreg Wastad in 1797, by an unknown artist. Courtesy of Carmarthen Museum.

First published 2007

Tempus Publishing Limited
The Mill, Brimscombe Port,
Stroud, Gloucestershire, GL5 2QG
www.tempus-publishing.com

British Library Cataloguing in Publication Data.
A catalogue record for this book is available from the British Library.

ISBN 978 0 7524 4010 1

Typesetting and origination by Tempus Publishing Limited
Printed in Great Britain

CONTENTS

In memory of my ancestors, all of whom lived within a few miles

of the invasion when it happened: Enoch Absalom (b. 1735),

Owain (b. 1786) and Dorothy (b. 1787) Absalom, Mary Adams,

John (b. 1779) and Mary Thomas, Henry (b. 1755) and

Anne (b. 1760) James, John (b. 1785) and Mary (b. 1791) Rees,

John and Anne Rees, Henry and Martha Phillip.

And this book is also for their very recent descendant:

Matilda Alice Thomas (b. 2 October 2005).

May she take pride in her inheritance.

About the Author

J.E. Thomas was born and brought up in Haverfordwest. He can trace his Pembrokeshire roots back to the seventeenth century, and in 1797 his great-great-grandparents were living as Pembrokeshire smallholders. He is Professor Emeritus at the University of Nottingham, and was, until his retirement in 1996, Senior Pro Vice Chancellor and Head of Department and Dean of the Faculty of Education. He has degrees from Oxford, London, York and Nottingham universities, and is the author of twelve books. He now lives in Nottingham.

Acknowledgements

To Hazel Mills, for her expertise in taking and reproducing many of the photographs in this book. Indeed the credit for the bulk of the illustrations in this book must go to her. I am indebted too for her interminable patience, when I lost my way in my computer. I am so very grateful to her.

To Josh Mills, for his translation of French, especially the biographical material about Pierre-Honoré Boudon de St. Amans, a French officer in the invasion force.

To Dilwyn and Jane Voyle, an honoured and ancient Pembrokeshire name, for much hospitality, and help with sources, when I was carrying out research in Haverfordwest. Dilwyn also went to the trouble of photographing the churches in Haverfordwest.

To Professor Nick Hewitt of the University of Nottingham, for arranging access to the story of St Amans, and for help with translation.

To Marie-Dominique Nivière, Conservateur du Musée des Beaux-Arts d'Agen for sending otherwise unobtainable material about St Amans.

To Joe McDonnell-Thomas for obtaining the regimental badge of the Pembrokeshire Yeomanry.

I would like to thank especially the staff of all the libraries, and archives which I used. Their readiness to help is universal, remarkable, and totally professional. In particular I am indebted to Miss N.J. Bosworth of the Pembrokeshire Record Office, who advised me about a range of problems, and drew my attention to material I would otherwise have missed.

List of Illustrations

Introduction

Pembrokeshire, the scene of the famous 'last invasion of Britain' at the end of the eighteenth century, was isolated and sparsely populated. In the first national census of 1801, it was recorded to have a population of 56,280. This reflected a steady growth of population in Wales throughout the eighteenth century, although the scale and timing of this growth has always been a matter of discussion amongst historians. In 1795, just before the first census taken in 1801, it was estimated that the population of the parish of Fishguard, the focus of this study, was some 2,800.[1] But even though the people of Pembrokeshire at the end of the eighteenth century were isolated, that isolation, and even the language barrier, did not mean that the common people were ignorant or unaware of events shaking the world. This premise is the underlying theme of this book. But firstly we look at how the people earned a living.

At that time there was some extractive industry in the county. There was not the amount of lead mining for which Carmarthenshire and Cardiganshire were so notable, but there was a seam of coal which ran from Nolton on the west coast to Saundersfoot in the east, which had been mined since the fourteenth century, and would continue to be operated until the 1950s. By 1700, coal had become the main export from the county, and by the end of that century was being exported as far afield as Europe. Charles Hassall, a person with whom we shall become familiar, noted that 'none of the rival collieries of South Wales are equal in quality with the Pembrokeshire coal'.[2] We shall go on to see how miners from Hook in central Pembrokeshire caused a riot, much under sung, and much underrated, during the starving years around the end of the eighteenth century. This riot is an important element in understanding the mood of the times.

There was some quarrying which, while not employing many people, was nevertheless of significance in those areas where it was carried out.[3] On the borders of Cardiganshire and Pembrokeshire there was a tinplate operation which seems to have begun in about 1764, the site being especially suitable because of the large quantity of wood to make charcoal, and the fact that the river Teifi was navigable. Later at the end of the eighteenth century, this venture came under the control of a wealthy Englishman, Sir Benjamin Hammet. In his day a considerable proportion of the local population, between 200–300 people, were employed in the works.[4]

As the county is on the coast, it is to be expected that people would be occupied in fishing. Visitors wrote about this, as they did about much local work, observing that it could be substantially improved. Writing about the catching of salmon in the Fishguard district, one critic in 1795 wrote that the people did not begin to harvest until the 'fish almost jump into the houses'.[5] Nevertheless, this was an important source of food for many people, and indeed in the coastal areas it was one of the staple meals, in an area which was very short of food. Yet, in spite of such criticism, at about the same time it is reported that there was an export market of salted salmon to London.[6] And, it was observed that oysters were exported from Milford Haven to London and Holland.[7] For the purposes of export, especially of coal, there was activity at several ports. Milford Haven, with its quite remarkable harbour, was already being described by Defoe in the 1720s as, 'the largest, richest and ... most flourishing town in South Wales except Carmarthen'.[8] Haverfordwest too was an important port, being able to handle ships of 200 tons, and was the scene of much commercial activity, and of course Fishguard was also notable for its shipping.

But the mainstay of life in Pembrokeshire was agriculture, and it was upon this which most people relied. According to Charles Hassall, who wrote an official report on agriculture in Pembrokeshire, it was mostly grossly inefficient at all levels, and he despairs at the reluctance of the farmers to improve their systems. For example, there was universal condemnation of the ploughs in use throughout west Wales. Hassall writes that: 'perhaps a more awkward unmeaning tool, is not to be found in any civilised country'.[9] Another visitor, writing in 1814, some twenty years after Hassall, observes that there are no 'models of greater antiq-uity': 'They may plume themselves with the idea, that they now use a plough the very *facsimile* of that described by Virgil nearly two thousand years ago'.[10]

Hassall, incidentally, is someone who features in an especially inflam-matory consequence of the invasion. This was the accusation that Lieutenant Colonel Knox, the commander of the Fishguard volunteers, was guilty of cowardice. But the two men had a complicated history, since both were Irish, and Knox's father had dismissed Hassall as his manager. It is also the case that the landowners of Pembrokeshire would never have accepted a rich and successful Irishman, especially one who had enough money to found a regiment – the Fishguard volunteers, who were in fact the biggest unit at the scene of the invasion: 191 against 43 of the Pembrokeshire Yeomanry. And he was seemingly resentful and difficult about supposed grievances. But such rich men flocked to Pembrokeshire, because of the richness of the land, especially in the south. The peasants depended on farming, and in this the women took a full part. As well as managing the house and taking part in all of the men's activities, the women, and the children too, tried hard in a desper-ate attempt to augment income by spinning.

Despite criticism by people like Hassall, there were pockets of excel-lence in Pembrokeshire. The county was noted for the quality of its horses, and Francis Jones records how, in 1778, Richard Vaughan of the immensely wealthy estate of Golden Grove in Carmarthenshire, sent his mares to Pembrokeshire to be covered by the fine stallions there.[11] One of the more colourful aspects of farming at the time, and probably one of the most profitable, was the 'droving' of cattle hundreds of miles from Pembrokeshire, and other parts of Wales to London and other cities. This phenomenon has been the source of many stories, and at the centre of them is the legendary drover and his famous Castlemartin 'black' cat-tle. Amongst their many critical jobs was the handling of money, often in substantial amounts. It was the drovers who established the famous bank called the Black Ox in Llandovery in 1799. We shall also see that they were an important, indeed vital communication channel between all classes of Pembrokeshire society and the outside world.

Although in recent years scholarly attention has been turned to the ordinary people, still not enough is made of the misery which was the hallmark of life in west Wales. For most of the people living there,

Pembrokeshire, and for that matter the whole of south west Wales, at the end of the eighteenth century was in a state of wretchedness and poverty from which there would be little relief until the beginning, or even the middle of the twentieth century. The evidence for this can be seen in the very many reports from visitors who, deprived of the opportunity to visit the continent because of the continental war, visited Wales, and were generally shocked at what they saw. As late as 1846, in a typical Pembrokeshire parish, Narbeth, life expectancy was 'not above 33 years as appears from the register'.[12]

Pembrokeshire was also a stronghold of nonconformity, and this was a source of much conflict, and would remain so until well into the twentieth century. It was so important, that the Duke of Rutland saw it as the explanation for what was reported as local disloyalty during the invasion. His version of events is generally seen as wrong, and his views as deriving from that hatred of dissenters which was characteristic of powerful people at the time. This antagonism on both sides also colours the standard version of the treason trials, consequent upon the invasion, in which local people were charged with very serious offences. This standard version is that as the prosecutions were abandoned, it is proof that the men were innocent, and were only prosecuted because they were nonconformists.

We will go on to see that the evidence of collusion between some local people and the invaders was strong: nor should this be a matter of surprise. We will see that there was much sympathy for, and much knowledge of the ideals of the French Revolution in Wales, and that there was little in the *status quo* which operated to the benefit of the poor. There is nothing to be ashamed of in the distrust of those in power, which is a constant theme in the conversations which Rutland recounts. This distrust also serves to reinforce the view that had the French had a better leader, and had their soldiers been better controlled, the course of events could have been very different, and a good deal more damaging, since the much proclaimed loyalty of local people was never really put to the test.

In February 1797, to the unutterable surprise of the British government and people, a force of mainly French, but also including Irish and American soldiers, (the commanding officer William Tate was an American) under the direction of the French Revolutionary government, invaded Pembrokeshire. This book will examine the reasons for this, the social state of Pembrokeshire, and more generally west Wales at the time, the events of the invasion, and the aftermath. Of central importance will be the distinguishing of fact from myth, since the history of the event is replete with legend, some of which is of questionable provenance. The historian Richard Fenton, who was born in Pembrokeshire, and who briefly discussed the invasion wrote that:

> The accounts which are given of it to the public are as various as the passions of the different narrators, now magnified beyond the bounds of probability, now lessened till they cease to possess any interest, where the truth of the narrative was sacrificed to party spirit, to indiscriminate and malignant censure on the one hand, and fulsome adulation on the other.[13]

The principal contention of this book is that Fenton is near the truth when he alleges that some accounts are 'magnified beyond the bounds of probability'. He might have felt totally justified in his opinion, had he seen the volumes on the subject printed since his death. Hyperbole is a signal feature of many such accounts.

Of especial interest in the attempt to sort out fact and fiction is the reliability of the particular oral history, upon which so much of the story of the invasion depends. Laws, for example, notes that the version of the events by H.L. Williams, upon which so much reliance has been placed as we shall go on to see, is dedicated to:

> Major Bowling, only surviving officer of the Castlemartin Yeomanry who was present at the surrender of the French troops on Goodwick Sands; while Peter Davies, innkeeper, and Owen Griffiths, schoolmaster, who served in the Fishguard Fencibles under Col. Knox, sign as having examined the account and found it correct.[14]

Even someone who was born in Fishguard only two years after the invasion, Reverend Henry Vincent, who was an antiquarian, was witness to the growth of fictional versions:

> In those days (of his childhood) hundreds were wont to crowd to the spot every summer when the natives had the opportunity of refreshing their memories, fighting their battles over again and spinning long yarns which they turned to a more speedy and in a pecuniary view, to a more profitable account than the webb (sic) of Penelope.[15]

So, can we believe the evidence of the people who were there, or more to the point the relation of events by people who met the people who were there? And can we trust the judgement of Welsh historians, who in turn have accepted such evidence? The views of the latter seem to be variously that the matter has been blown out of all proportion, or that it was a great victory, and above all, that the integrity of the local people must remain intact. This book sets out to establish that the invasion was a serious matter, and that the integrity of the people is preserved, not by mass support for the authorities, but by their evident hesitation in supporting the squires.

As to the invasion, the seriousness of the event has often been dismissed. One does not have to look far to find writers who would support Gwyn A. Williams who wrote of it as a 'comic opera landing.'[16] Salmon, one of those with an intimate knowledge of the documentation and the events sums up his view in a sentence: 'the invasion of Pembrokeshire was a farce'.[17] At the other extreme the verdict has been that the victory over the invader was the consequence of acts of bravery by the defending forces and the local population, and that the country, or some of it, was saved from terrible depredation and suffering. Or that in the opinion of someone who was alive in the district at the time, the historian Richard Fenton, the victorious outcome derived from the fact that the French were intoxicated, and out of control. But that nevertheless:

> For certain it is, had they availed themselves of the first moments of alarm, debate, and indecision, the ravage, without much hazard to themselves, they might have committed is incalculable. Fishguard, a place totally incompetent to oppose such a force, with all its wealth, its shipping shut up at the time benepped in her harbour, was in sight, and might have become an easy prey: nay, all the country, even to the opulent town of Haverfordwest, might have felt the force of their arms before they could have received any material check.[18]

So the invasion is an event which invites the sorting of fact from fiction. With this in mind, two books in particular should be mentioned. The first is 'The last invasion of Britain' by E.H. Stuart Jones. Published in 1950, this is the first scholarly account, which suffers slightly from the historic tendency of writing on the invasion to overstate the 'loyalty' of local people, and to regard as grossly unfair the reported experience of those who were there, that such 'loyalty' was uncertain, and could not be assumed or guaranteed:

> It is difficult to think that the French Revolution, at this stage, could have made any appeal to the peace-loving inhabitants of Pencaer. They would have been horrified by the Terror and the religious persecutions, still fresh in their minds. The more knowledgeable of them would not have been impelled towards the gang of regicides who composed the Directory, for even the austere and Calvinistic Carnot had voted for the death of King Louis XVI. They would have felt no appeal in the 'new' religion of Larevellière, Lépeaux, protector of the Theophilanthropists. The scandalous intrigues of the pleasure-loving, *déclassé*, nobleman Paul Barras with Thérèse Cabarrus, the legal wife of the citizen Tallien, would have shocked their rigid code of morals.[19]

It goes without saying that Jones' assessment of the attitudes of the people is highly speculative, and it will be shown to be hardly shared by many educated people, especially nonconformists.

The second text is called by the dramatic and lengthy title:

> An authentic account of the invasion by the French troops, (under the Command of General Tate) on Carrig Gwasted Point near Fishguard, on Wednesday, the 22nd Day of February, 1797, and their surrender to the forces of His Britannic Majesty, on Goodwick Sands, on February, the 24th of February; Likewise, some occurrences connected therewith, never before published.

The author was 'A native of the Principality' and in the first edition of August 1842 signs himself as H.L. Ap Gwilym. In the second edition of 1853, he signs himself H.L. Williams. In passing it may be noted that even the title contains two mistakes: Tate was not a General and 'Carrig Gwasted' is arguably misspelt. Despite the guarantees of its authenticity by people who took part over forty years before it was written, the book contains blatant inaccuracies. But more than that, it is the first to propagate chronic myths, for which no authority seems to exist, which were seized upon, and were to become locked into subsequent accounts.

This is remarkable when it is borne in mind that Williams does not draw upon any documentary sources, and relies entirely upon hearsay. As Rose points out, there is no evidence for the assumption by Salmon, and repeated by Stuart Jones, that he was a member of the Fishguard volunteers at the time of the attack. Indeed Williams does not make the claim, although in his second edition he describes himself as Lieutenant in the Fishguard volunteers.[20]

This book will reassess what is commonly regarded as received and indubitable knowledge. It will emphasise the social context and relationships in Pembrokeshire which are essential to the understanding of the period. Events in France will be discussed, and the critical influence of the French Revolution on Wales will be emphasised. There will be a description and reassessment of the course of events, and the curiosities of the aftermath. Throughout I will also seek to distinguish fact from fiction without setting out to be iconoclastic for its own sake.

The People of Pembrokeshire in 1797

To understand the events surrounding the invasion, it is necessary to understand the structure and dynamics of Pembrokeshire society at the time. Such awareness will help in the understanding of what would otherwise appear to be inexplicable happenings. These include, and these are only examples, the failure of the defending forces to engage the invaders; the excessive insistence, especially by later writers, on the loyalty of local people to the Crown and the government; the paradox that some local people were charged with treason, and others nearly so; the hounding of Thomas Knox, the commanding officer of the Fishguard Volunteers; and the creation of a rich web of legend and myth for which there is little or no evidence. Taken in isolation many of these episodes make no sense, but it is in the social and political context that explanations can be found. And at the heart of it all are the social divisions, barriers and hostility which dominated the lives, not only of Pembrokeshire people, but of those who lived in west Wales, and were observed generally throughout Wales. At the top of the hierarchy were the squires.

At the end of the eighteenth century there was in Pembrokeshire a small group of landowners who had, over the previous 100 years, accumulated considerable wealth. Some of these were active in the events of the invasion. By contrast, the peasantry were amongst the poorest, and most wretched in the whole of Britain. At the time, because of the war with France, any of the customary, familiar travel to Europe by those British people who could afford it was impossible, and so instead they travelled to remote parts of Britain, including Wales, in particular west Wales. They wrote accounts, often detailed, of their journeys, and as we shall go on to see, a common theme was the squalor of the lives of the poor in Pembrokeshire, a common unfavourable comparison being made with the state of the common people in Ireland. An arresting and illuminating statistic, is that of the nineteen workhouses in Wales, no fewer than eleven were in Pembrokeshire.[1] It is possible to regard this figure as evidence of 'progress', in that provision was being made, but in any event the conditions in them were hardly a matter of congratulation. In 1800 a magistrate made a visit to a poorhouse in Johnston, which is situated between Haverfordwest and Milford, and reported that it was:

> In a very ruinous state, the Roof being much out of Repair and the House filthy and unhealthy in a great degree then having a quantity of Ashes and dirt in it and in some parts open at the Roof, and by no means fit and proper for the Reception of the Poor I found removal to and then placed there six persons … one Bed only in the said House … and not even a bit of straw or anything else whereon the other Poor Persons could lay their Heads … the said House in its present state is not fit for Human Beings.[2]

The desperate situation of the poor people of Pembrokeshire was shared by their neighbours in Cardiganshire and Carmarthenshire, and for that matter throughout Wales. To add to everything else: 'There is some indication that the old tradition of dispensing hospitality at mansions was in decline in the late eighteenth century, however, at a time when the needs of the poor were growing ever more clamorous.'[3]

In contrast, the wealth of the landowners may be exemplified by some account of the background and wealth of some of the principal actors in the invasion drama of 1797. Richard Philips who had recently been created Lord Milford, of Picton Castle near Haverfordwest, John Campbell also recently ennobled as Baron Cawdor, of Stackpole Court, near Pembroke; Dudley Ackland of Boulston; James Ackland of Llanion; Thomas Knox of Minwear which is sometimes spelled Minwere, both near Haverfordwest; and John Colby of variously spelt Ffynone or Fynone or Ffynnone. Such variations in the spelling of Welsh place names is constant and confusing; thus two experts disagree about this particular spelling. The correct spelling is Ffynnon, according to B.G. Charles, or Ffynone, as argued by Baker-Jones:

> In passing, it may be worth noting that the name Ffynone has been thus spelt for centuries and represents the local pronunciation of the orthographically correct

form "Ffynhonnau" ... within yards of the present Ffynone mansion there are about half a dozen springs or wells, which may have explained its name.[4]

The Philips family was one of the earliest recorded in Pembrokeshire, and their wealth and distinction led to John Philips being literally forced to accept a baronetcy in 1621, despite his protests that he could not afford it. From that point and throughout the eighteenth century, the family accumulated considerable wealth, a process which continued during the nineteenth century. In 1793 the Picton estate brought in an income of £5,600 annually.[5] By 1883 the estate 'consisted of 23,054 acres in Pembrokeshire and Carmarthenshire worth £23,815 a year.'[6] At the time of the invasion Sir Richard Philips had just been made a baron in the Irish peerage, (in 1776) as a 'solatium' (consolation) because he had been refused permission to make a roadway up to his house overlooking St James' park in London. In 1797 he was the Whig member of Parliament for the county of Pembroke, and Lord Lieutenant of Haverfordwest. He was, however, suffering so badly from gout that when the French landed he had to relinquish command of the local forces, which was part of his responsibility as Lord Lieutenant.

The man who took over as overall commander of the local forces which were pitted against the French, was John Campbell, by then Baron Cawdor of Castlemartin. Campbell was a classic example of the landlords of the Welsh countryside, notably in that he was not entirely of Welsh extraction. He was mainly Scottish, his ancestor, Sir Alexander, in 1689, having married the heir to the Lort estates in south Pembrokeshire, thus gaining a considerable inheritance. Like Lord Milford, at the end of the eighteenth century he was possessed of enormous wealth and wielded formidable power in the counties of Pembrokeshire and Carmarthenshire. In 1725 the Stackpole[7] estate was worth £2,800, but by 1793 it brought in an income of £15,000 a year, which was the largest estate income in south west Wales.[8] This was in the most fertile part of Pembrokeshire, and was 'some 14 miles in length and of various breadths from 7 to 14 ... containing about 16,000 acres'. Hassall, who wrote about these details, added that in south Pembrokeshire 'the property of this valuable land is in very few hands'.[9] He added to his fortune when, to the surprise of many, especially the relatives of the deceased, he was left the enormous Vaughan estate of Golden Grove in Carmarthenshire. He was created Baron Cawdor in the Irish peerage because he changed

his political allegiance, and supported Pitt's unpopular war policy. And so
he was 'part of an unprecedentedly large list of nominations' which had
to be accepted by George III.[10]

Dudley Ackland was born in Philadelphia in 1748, but his ancestors
came from Devon. He had held the rank of Major in the 91st Regiment
of Foot. Some years after moving to Pembrokeshire he bought the
Boulston estate in 1797, and he built a new house, as the original mansion was ruined. This was another of the estates which historically had
belonged to the powerful Wogan family, who had for several hundred
years dominated Pembrokeshire public life. The last of this family to live
there was Anne Wogan, who, although married, died childless in 1715.
Fenton stayed with Ackland on his 'Tour' and pronounced of Boulston
that: 'it would be difficult to have fixed on a spot involving so many
ingredients of beauty, consequence and comfort ... nor would the
recorded hospitality of the old, the theme of bards, suffer any disparage-
ment by a comparison with the new.' He also expressed his gratitude for
having been allowed to open a 'very large tumulus' on his land.[11]

Like so many of the landowners in Pembrokeshire, and throughout
Wales, Dudley Ackland was not local or Welsh. He was not a landowner
on such a large scale as some, but nevertheless wielded great power and
as a major in the Pembrokeshire Yeomanry, he figured prominently in
the events surrounding the invasion. He was also remarkable in that
he showed some sympathy for the plight of the poor, and he wrote to
Cawdor on one occasion when there were protests over the inability
of the people to buy corn, to express the hope that they would not be
'brought to the disagreeable necessity of firing upon our poor creatures'.[12]
He may even have resigned, or threatened to resign his commission in
the Pembrokeshire Yeomanry, because of disapproval of the repression
which was the central duty of Yeomanry everywhere.[13] And he wrote to
Cawdor from Pembroke on 10 March with a resolution, signed by 'all
the principal people here', notifying him that the price of a number of
goods had been capped, much to Cawdor's annoyance.[14]

Another Ackland, Captain James Ackland was the commanding officer
of the Pembroke Volunteers. He had estates at Llanion near Pembroke,
and at Earwear (Amroth Castle). Ackland was one of the last to live at
Llanion, since by 1811 Fenton wrote that it was 'unroofed and suffered
to fall into decay.'[15] Amroth Castle was altogether grander. Before 1798
it was taken possession of by Ackland, who built a new 'most desirable

mansion, possessing every appendage of luxury and convenience'.[16] So Ackland, like the other prominent officers, was very wealthy.

Thomas Knox was to prove a very controversial figure. His father, William, had been Under Secretary of State for America, and arrived in Pembrokeshire with a considerable fortune and bought two estates, those of Llanstinan in the north, and Slebech in the south. Llanstinan was another of the many ancestral homes of one of the most powerful families in Pembrokeshire since the middle ages, the Wogans. Throughout the eighteenth century however, the family proved increasingly infertile, and so in 1710 their property fell into the hands of their kinsmen, the Symmons. John Symmons was the last of his family to own the estate, and also that of Slebech, but, as again was not uncommon he overspent, and had to sell towards the end of the eighteenth century, in this case to Knox.

The view has been expressed that Knox was a bitter man, because he felt that he had not properly been rewarded for his public service, but he did open the first post office in Fishguard, set up the first county agricultural society, and established the first packet service from Milford to Waterford, and was very active in advancing progress in the county in other ways.[17] When war was declared with France in 1793 he raised, and of course paid for, a regiment of 'Fencible Infantry', the nature of which will be discussed later. His son Thomas was appointed Commanding Officer, and when the invasion came, the Fishguard 'Fencibles' produced the largest force. But Thomas Knox was later to be the subject of allegations that he had acted in a cowardly fashion, and the matter was to end in the ruination of his family.

Colonel John Colby had his estate at Ffynnon: another very old Pembrokeshire estate. In 1752 it was bought by the Colby family, and in 1779 it passed to John Colby, and like so many of the local landowners of the day, he was wealthy enough to build a much more impressive house in about 1795 and 'by the turn of the [eighteenth] century the mansion house of Ffynone was one of the finest in the county'.[18] At the time of the invasion he was a Lieutenant Colonel, and Commanding Officer of the Pembrokeshire militia, to which post he had been appointed by his brother-in-law, Sir Hugh Owen, the Lord Lieutenant. In 1797 Colby was aged about forty-six. His career was not free of trouble, since, like Knox, but in a different cause, there was a move to have him court-martialled. The problem arose during a tour of duty by the Militia in Ireland in

1799. It would appear that at the end of the six month tour, at the behest of his superiors, Colby suggested that the tour should be extended, but the men were unwilling to do so. Not only that, some of his officers moved to have him punished. They:

> alleged that when the request was made for the Regiment to consider staying longer in Ireland, Colby, without consulting them took the request directly to the other ranks and was rebuffed. They felt aggrieved at being bypassed, and were of the opinion that, had they been given an opportunity to negotiate, the outcome would have been different.

As a consequence Colby resigned his command of the regiment.[19] Nevertheless, he continued his public career, being made Commanding Officer of the Independent Pembrokeshire Corps of Yeomanry in 1805 and in 1807 he was High Sheriff for Pembrokeshire.[20]

With so much wealth and power, the lives of the Pembrokeshire land-owners were full and prosperous. Their expensive education led them to expect luxury and to regard themselves as national figures rather than local magnates. The most important families began formal education in public schools. Hugh Owen of Orielton, near Pembroke, for example, went to Eton in 1793.[21] The more modest, but comfortably off families, such as that of Sir Thomas Picton went to the local, well established Grammar Schools, in his case Haverfordwest. From there they went either to university, usually Oxford which had a strong Welsh connection, Cambridge, or to one of the Inns of Court. Their time in such institutions was not invariably marked by the wastrel behaviour which is the common stereotype of the eighteenth-century landed classes, although there is plenty of evidence to support said stereotype. Howell singles out the case of Erasmus Philips of Picton who, in the diary he kept at Pembroke College Oxford, recorded that while spending his time 'in the gentlemanly pursuits of fox-hunting, fishing, watching horse-racing and riding', he also 'had a great love for books and music'.[22]

The mansions of the west Wales squires at the end of the eighteenth century attracted much comment and admiration. Although modest compared with the finest in England, their houses and environs were grand enough. In Cardiganshire, a county which was notably desperate for food at the time, and an area of extreme poverty, a visitor to Hafod, the home of Thomas Johnes in 1798 wrote: 'The surprise is scarcely to be described with which his highly ornamental territory burst upon our view, teeming with every elegance of art and nature, and rising, like another paradise, in the midst of a profound desert.'[23]

In Pembrokeshire the same kinds of observations were made. In 1798 Stackpole Court was deemed to be 'a noble mansion surrounded with fine groves and growing plantations'.[24] In addition they had town houses in Haverfordwest and London. They gambled (often disastrously); raced horses; hunted (Milford and Cawdor had their own packs); went to seemingly interminable balls; shot game; and watched people, dogs, and cocks fight. Above all they visited each other, and in the course of such visits 'the consumption of food and wine was on a grand scale'.[25] In addition to such excess, it was on these occasions that they indulged their passion for gambling. As well as this, they listened to music, played billiards and talked.

They were, in addition, members of Parliament, governors of town castles, sheriffs, patrons of church livings, and justices of the peace, dispensing justice as they conceived it to be. With rare exceptions, Cawdor and Squire John Mirehouse of Brownslade being two, the gentry were not philanthropists, and were not generous to their tenants and labourers. It was said of Mirehouse, for example that he was one: 'who furnished their cottagers with necessary articles at the ordinary rate during the scarcity ... he is esteemed one of the best gentlemen farmers in the kingdom.'[26]

Mirehouse's estate at Brownslade near Angle, was recognised as being altogether exceptional. His reclaiming of land was such a success that in 1800 he was awarded the Gold Medal of the Society for the Encouragement of Arts, Science and Commerce.[27]

More usual was the assessment given when the lower orders had the rare opportunity to evaluate the squirearchy. People giving evidence to the commissioners who inspected educational provision in Wales in the 1840s, claimed that in south Pembrokeshire, 'the landed proprietors are non-resident and contribute nothing to schools'.[28] Similarly, in Carmarthenshire it was claimed that 'the neighbouring gentry have done nothing at all towards promoting education', [29] although another witness excepted Cawdor from this rule.[30] Even William Knox had his critics in spite of the fact that he did a lot to improve the county, and helped the starving population. In July 1795, for instance, he wrote to the Duke of Portland, asking for corn to be dispatched from Scotland saying that,

'I will be answerable for the first cost'.[31] One critic was especially offensive about Knox's enclosure of land – another cause of widespread rioting.
Knox was 'an Irish wolf who have not the look of a man engaged in
tyrannical barbarous proceedings'.[32]

There was no sign of an end to the luxurious life of the squirearchy at the end of the eighteenth century, which indeed was at its peak.
But as always there were those who saw deterioration. In his account
of Pembrokeshire published in 1811, Fenton bewails what he sees as
the decay of much of traditional gentry life: 'I cannot help observing,
that here, to excite the most melancholy reflections, at every mile you
meet a mansion degradingly altered, deserted or in ruins; and like its
former inhabitants, now only remembered by name; which within the
last century was the rendezvous of beauty, wit, and festivity.'[33] Fenton is,
of course, correct in describing how families – through profligacy, bad
luck, or that curious phenomenon of the Welsh gentry, infertility – failed
to maintain or lost their estates, or witnessed themselves as the last of
the line. But it is important to stress that not only was the Welsh squirearchy at the period of the invasion very prosperous, but they enjoyed a
prosperity which was to be much enhanced in the nineteenth century.
Indeed there was little challenge to their political or financial power,
until the advent of reforming legislation at the end of that century, and
into the twentieth.

The extent of the wealth and the influence of the gentry and their
mode of living have been dwelt upon at some length, so that the contrast between their position and that of the farmers and peasants may be
more clearly seen. It provides a vital background to understanding some
of the less often (since controversial), reported events surrounding the
invasion.

The farmers were a very mixed group, in terms of the size of their
holdings and their wealth. There was a fairly prosperous group who were
termed Yeomen. But a safe generalisation would be that there was often
a very thin division between them and the labourers they employed.
This was indeed so thin that a slight misfortune could propel the tenant
farmer into the ranks of the labourers. Much of the instability underlying this can be traced to the system of tenure in Pembrokeshire, as in
other counties. Although some farmers held long leases, for eighty or
ninety-nine years, or even for life, 'by far the most common type of lease
granted on the Pembrokeshire estates during the eighteenth century was

that for a term of three lives, and the life of the survivor, either lessor or lessee'. Howell sets out the variations in the arrangements.[34] The effect of these short term leases can be imagined. Farmers were reluctant to improve their estates in case the landlord might not renew the lease when it ended, choosing instead to seek another tenant who would, of course pay a higher rent. Howell points out that in the last quarter of the eighteenth century, the rents on the Pembrokeshire estates rose, and he gives as an example those of Lord Milford's Picton Castle estate. At that time, when leases expired here: 'rents were raised to double and even treble their previous levels'.[35] At the very time of the invasion, as well as the especial raising of rents, there was inflation because of the war, and a succession of especially bad harvests.

The consequence of this system of tenure was that there was no incentive; in fact there was a *disincentive* to improve. The occasional landowner realised this. One was John Mirehouse of Brownslade, already mentioned as exceptional, who 'loudly advocated a one-life term'.[36] Howell sets out the advantages. It was believed that this would concentrate the mind of the tenant, and would also remove the danger that a good farmer's successor might be no good at all – a considerable advantage for the owner.

In an overview of Pembrokeshire society, Walter Davies, who was very much what would today be called an 'establishment figure', sets the scene. He wrote in 1814, about a world that had not changed for at least 150 years, of a 'feudal connection' and of 'numerous instances, in the Dimetian Counties of Cardigan, Pembroke, and Caermarthen' where: 'Labourers and their families may be considered as heirlooms or appendages to the farms, to work all the year round, and one year after another, at a fixed low rate per day without victuals.'[37]

The low pay and the hard work was also a matter of constant comment. This was made by visitors who had contact with lead miners, coal miners, or agricultural workers. But perhaps the feature of life which most startled the visitor to Pembrokeshire, and indeed to west Wales generally, was the squalor of the housing, not only at the end of the eighteenth century, but throughout the whole length of the nineteenth. Looking at cottages near Haverfordwest at the end of the eighteenth century, Arthur Young expressed the opinion of many other visitors when he wrote that these 'were not a whit better than Irish cabins, without an equal show of pigs, poultry and cows'.[38] Twiston Davies and Edwards agreed, only differing from Young by adding that some cottages did have a pig, and this 'one pig in many Welsh cottages did, indeed, follow the Irish fashion and lie before the hearth, with the children playing around him.' It should be added that the family could not afford to eat the pig; it was usually sold. There is no disagreement about the accommodation of the poor:

> A mud cabin such as was common in some parts of Pembrokeshire, one liv-
> ing-room with a dark inner recess to serve as a bedroom, a hole in the roof
> to let out smoke, a single rushlight when darkness fell, inadequate food, fever
> and disease without any hope of skilled nursing, and at the end the grudging
> help of the parish. Wretched, degraded creatures …[39]

What emphasises the wretchedness of the life of the people of west Wales at the end of the eighteenth century, is the fact that there was no improvement whatsoever in the nineteenth. In the early 1840s Carmarthenshire and Pembrokeshire saw the eruption of protest which has since been called the Rebecca Riots, so called because the rioters, moving about by night, wore women's clothes, and because they used a text from Genesis 24:60: 'And they blessed Rebekah and said unto her, Let thy seed possess the gates of those which hate thee.' Their target was the hated tollgates. The rioters were very powerful indeed, and well organised. Their activities soon included attacks on workhouses, tithe owners, and other symbols of what they perceived to be oppression. The failure of the Yeomanry to find them, never mind stop them, caused regular soldiers to be sent under an officer, Colonel James Love, whose capability may be gauged from the fact that at the end of his career he was a General. Yet the authorities were so frustrated by their inability to apprehend Rebecca that there was a demand from the Home Secretary for Love's removal and the installation of a much larger force, 'of 1800 men, a regiment of cavalry and a demi brigade of guns'.[40] This was exac-erbated by *The Times'* report that 'the government are pouring in troops' but 'they laugh at the display of power by the government'. The riots were reported upon for *The Times* by Thomas Campbell Foster, and he was outraged at the condition under which people lived:

> I entered several labourer's cottages by the roadside, out of curiosity to see the
> actual condition of the people, and found them mud hovels, the floors of mud
> and full of holes, without chairs or tables, generally half filled with peat packed
> up in every corner. Beds there were none: nothing but loose straw and filthy

rags upon them. Peat fires on the floor in a corner filling the cottages with smoke, and three or four children huddled around them. In the most miserable part of St. Giles, in no part of England, did I ever witness such abject poverty.[41]

As might be expected, the food of the peasants was consonant with their housing. Hassall tells us that in Pembrokeshire the labourers lived on cheese, bread, milk, and vegetables, herrings and poor quality veal in season, and that by midsummer the barley was finished, and grain that was brought in was so dear that the people were 'reduced to a state of distress, which calls aloud for the assistance of the affluent'.[42]

In 1846, the provocative and much maligned 'Blue Books', the reports on education, continued the dismal litany of misery. In Clarbeston, Pembrokeshire, 'the labourers were wretchedly poor'[43] while in Marloes, not very far away, 'the houses were generally struggling and dilapidated, often partially unthatched: several are wholly in ruins and deserted'.[44] As the century went on the landowners became increasingly wealthy while the situation of the common people remained perilous. Published around 1867 was a contemporary description of life in Cilgerran, which is very near to Fishguard:

> The cottages, or rather hovels, in which the farm labourers dwell are squalidly wretched, and unfit for human habitation … [their wage] is not sufficient to maintain a wife and family; and how they do it honestly to me is a most perplexing mystery.[5]

A *hundred* years after the invasion, a witness giving evidence to a royal commission said that he had worked on his father's farm for twenty-five or thirty years. Breakfast was barley bread and a little butter and skimmed milk. Dinner might be rice and milk, a little bread and butter, and sometimes potatoes or bacon or cabbage. He would eat fresh meat three or four times a year, or a fowl or rabbit more often. At 7 p.m. a piece of barley bread sometimes of 'tail wheat' and butter and tea. 'A bit of bread and butter' would be supper before bed at 9 p.m. When asked if things were any better nowadays, he replied that they were the same except that he got some wholemeal bread.[46]

Yet there are reports of the remarkable way the peasantry coped, and maintained some degree of optimism. In 1803 a group of travellers were lost near Pembroke. Calling at a cottage, they were invited in by some miners. It will be remembered that coal mining was significant in the county at the time. 'Although in the exterior repulsive as their cheerless occupation, their hearts were not estranged from sensations of benevolence'. One said that, 'mother can give you a drop of good mead, and some decentish bread and butter'. She, in turn, said they were thankful for a good harvest, since the previous year, 'many of her neighbours died outright of hunger'. In spite of their poverty, and the manifest wealth of their visitors, she was reluctant to accept a gift.[47] Incidentally, such contact with miners seems to have been a salutary experience for visitors. Another wrote:

> Witnessing some of these poor creatures ascending out of the pits, just emerging *ab inferis ad lucem*, as black and forbidding in their aspect as the region they had just left, afforded us abundant reason to reflect on the obligations we were to a kind Providence, in not being obliged to earn the necessaries of life so far from the surface we trod on, and exempt also from the numerous accidents to which these our fellow creatures are exposed.[48]

Despite the enormous anger that the Blue Books excited, especially amongst the nonconformist oligarchy which was so powerful, there is much in the Reports which are a credit to the poor. Much is said, for example, about how they did their best to keep themselves and their homes clean and tidy. And very common is their enthusiasm for education, as this example from the small parish of Camrose in Pembrokeshire shows:

> People in the parish seemed all very anxious to educate their children if they had the means. The labouring classes were exceedingly poor. Wages were very low, and scarcely amounted to what would support them and their families, setting aside education, though they live upon a very poor and coarse diet.[49]

Although the patience of the common people is, in retrospect quite phenomenal, it was not inexhaustible. The discontent of the people, throughout Britain, was expressed in rioting. There were riots over politics, the enclosure of common land, and over religion. In Carmarthen, an especially turbulent town, one of many political riots took place in 1755, with the sheriff reporting that the town would be in flames, and that 'there are five hundred separate fellows come to town from

Pembrokeshire and other places, arm'd with firearms and quarter pieces, and, I am told, ship guns'. In this riot, as in many others, people were killed.[50] But the main cause of rioting was the shortage of corn, which was usually, if not invariably due to bad harvests, followed by a complex of racketeering by merchants. There were several varieties of this. They could 'forestall', which involved buying before the commodity was generally available for sale. There was 'engrossing', which was buying in huge quantities as a preliminary to 'regrating', which was selling on at a profit. In all such matters Wales was no exception. There were serious corn riots in as many as twelve years of the eighteenth century up to 1789.

In the case of Pembrokeshire, in 1740 a ship was attacked in Pembroke, and the corn removed. The rioters took it to market, and demanded that it be sold at a fair price. A threat followed to burn the town. Lord Dynevor wrote, in March 1795, reporting bread riots in Haverfordwest and Narberth.[52] One which has always attracted the attention of writers, albeit briefly, was a riot in Haverfordwest of colliers from Hook in 1795. This was, of course, just two years before the invasion, and should be seen as a much more accurate barometer of the feeling of local people than the wishful guesswork of Victorian commentators on their discipline and loyalty.

At the time, Haverfordwest was not only an important town, but also a substantial port, which could accommodate ships of up to 200 tons. Rev. Dr John Philips, a squire, rector, magistrate, and one of the Chairmen of the Quarter Sessions, sent an account to the Home Secretary about what happened.[53] On 17 August 1795, he was told that miners from the small village of Hook were going to board a sloop carrying butter from Haverfordwest to Bristol. This would happen at Hook, and Philips arranged for a tender to escort the sloop from Hook to Milford Haven. This was arranged with Captain Longcroft, who held the naval appointment in Milford of Regulating Officer, which meant that he *inter alia* organised the press gang. We shall encounter Longcroft later, since he figures prominently as the leader of a naval detachment in the invasion.

Early the next day, as Philips had arranged, fifty fully-armed men of the Carmarthen militia were in place in High Street, Haverfordwest, and they replied to a plea from some women to do them no harm that, 'they should do their duty'. At about midday, the colliers appeared: 'a great crowd of men women and children with oaken bludgeons coming

down the High Street bawling out "One for all, One for all'". Scuffles
then broke out with Philips trying to seize colliers, women – 'perfect
Furies' – hitting him, and colliers lashing out with their clubs. One mili-
tiaman ran at one with his bayonet, and would have killed him but for
the intervention of a clergyman. One woman was heard to shout 'that
in less than a twelvemonth she would see the downfall of all clergy and
of every rich person'. The Militia lined up, and were ordered to 'ram
the balls well that every shot might do execution'. When the Riot Act
was read the miners ran away. The next day a lighter man, who allegedly
had beaten somebody who had refused to join in the riot, appeared
in Haverfordwest. He was promptly arrested by Longcroft's press gang,
taken to Pembroke by thirty militia, and put on a ship. The situation
remained tense, and Colonel Knox was asked to bring his Volunteers to
keep order. He brought 100 men, and they remained for a week before
the authorities could be sure that the town was peaceful. Knox was
sufficiently pleased to write an account to the Duke of Portland who
expressed his approval.[54] This episode showed the importance of both
militia and volunteers in putting down civil discontent in the absence of
regular soldiers.

This was by no means the end of rioting in Pembrokeshire, nor the
last that was heard of Rev. Philips, or the miners. In 1796 there were
riots around St David's, especially interesting later when we deal with
the supposed response from the people of that neighbourhood to the
news of the invasion. In 1800–01 there was a great stir in Newport, very
near to Fishguard, because the mayor, John Ladd, himself led the riots.
At about the same time miners threatened to burn down Picton castle causing Lord Milford to seek refuge in London. As to Philips, his
bravado facing the Hook miners later seems to have deserted him. In
April 1800 he wrote a much less triumphant letter to the Duke of
Portland:

> The magistrates this day assembled at the Quarter Sessions complained to me
> that they had lately received several anonymous letters threatening to burn
> down their houses and to destroy all their property. They desired me as their
> Chairman to represent the case to your Grace as they really now are afraid of
> their lives. I have inclosed a letter which was sent to me & two others which
> were sent to Mr. Wright another of our Pembrokeshire magistrates. I should
> imagine that if Government would advertise a reward for the discovery of

the writers, it would strike a terror into them. But I submit it to your Grace's better judgement, what step is best to be taken.[55]

These disturbances carried on throughout the nineteenth century. One episode, which must be described as paradoxical, occurred in Fishguard in January 1827. There was serious rioting when the townspeople tried to prevent the export of corn - the old familiar grievance. The Lord Lieutenant sent in the Yeomanry to suppress the people, who had supposedly been so loyal only thirty years before.

As well as taking things into their own hands by purloining corn and other produce destined for export, the common people along the Pembrokeshire coast were notorious for their smuggling. This could be hugely profitable, and a great temptation to a people who did not even have enough to eat, never mind any luxuries. As well as the legendary spirits and tobacco, Pembrokeshire was especially noted for the smuggling of salt. At that time it was subject to a heavy duty, and was, of course, highly prized as a preservative for food. The association of the county with this activity is noted in a report from a body called the Salt Commissioners in February 1796:

> The practice of smuggling salt on the coast of Wales is chiefly confined to those parts of it that lay between St. David's Head near the entrance of Milford Haven, and Cardigan Bay inclusive, that little or no smuggling of that article exists on the northward or southward of those places … to prevent this it will be necessary for your officers on that coast to keep a diligent lookout … the landing generally takes place in the night time protected by such numerous gangs of smugglers as make it impossible for the officers to appear. Cruisers at sea will be more likely to check the practice in some degree, provided that are kept in a state of active cruising.[56]

Oddly enough, the curbing of smuggling was a particular interest of Lord Cawdor's. In fact his apparent disapproval of it marks him out from the generality of the squirearchy, who famously colluded with and benefited from the practice. On at least one occasion in 1801 he went to Tenby with the local collector in a cutter commanded by John Hopkins who had joined his forces in 1797, when they noticed a ship at anchor. They decided the ship was a smuggler, and having landed, found some marks of horses. They found the trappings of the spirit trade, and at one place there was 'a strong smell of liquor'. They went on to Trewent Mill and came across some liquor, left out, 'in an attempt to distract the Speedwell's mariners from their rummaging'.[57]

Later in 1801, Cawdor's enthusiasm for chasing smugglers was to lead him into some danger in the same district. The smugglers were notoriously violent if cornered, as he was to discover. In a letter dated 18 November, Lady Cawdor reported what had happened. He had learned that a vessel with smuggled goods was going to land in the bay of Freshwater East. He and three men went down to the beach, and discovered casks there, which had been abandoned by the smugglers. One of the party was sent to bring carts to take away the booty, but the smugglers now realised that there were only a few men with Cawdor, and furthermore, that they, 'were perfectly unarmed'. They returned to the shore, and took the casks back to their vessel. Cawdor realised that he could do nothing and was returning to his home, when he was attacked, 'by some of these horrible desperate villains':

> Two of them fell upon Lord C, one armed with a great bludgeon, the other with a large poker with which he hit Lord C a violent blow on his arm. Lord C jumped off his horse and tried to catch hold of him, when another came behind and knocked him down with a blow on his head. In this situation with both these men thumping him, it is most fortunate he was so little stunned as to be able to get up and twist the poker out of the man's hand, with which he hit one of them, and then they both ran away.

They did manage to capture one of the smugglers, but:

> A short time after the house was surrounded by about thirty of the gang, people of the country armed with bludgeons, who immediately rescued their comrade ... Lord C has been very ill in consequence: he kept his bed all day yesterday, and was twice blooded but, thank God, he is so much better tonight I felt quite easy about him.[58]

Clearly these smugglers were not to be trifled with, nor were they unwilling to attack one of the most important squires in the county. It is apparent too, that they could rely on support from the 'people of the country'. It is not known whether or not Cawdor left the dangerous business of catching smugglers to the professionals after this.

Closely related to this coastal crime were wrecking and the robbing of wrecked ships. Whole communities would turn out to seize a cargo, and the authorities were usually powerless to stop them. There was an interesting twist to this when the invasion happened. A Portuguese ship had been wrecked off Fishguard, and its cargo of wine was in every home in the district. We shall see that the invaders drank too much of it.

Looking precisely at the Fishguard area, firstly in respect of its defences, there was a fort in a very powerful position overlooking the bay. However on 2 March 1795 Gwynne Vaughan, the governor of Fishguard fort, wrote to London to point out how little powder was in the fort, and asked for more, 'as the bay and harbour of Fishguard is extremely well calculated to afford shelter to all vessels navigating the Irish Channel'. He reminds the reader that in 1779 before the fort was built (in 1781) the *Black Prince* (a privateer) did so, shelled the town, and took and ransomed seventeen of the vessels lying there.[59] Stuart Jones though writes that, 'the captain of an armed smuggler kept up a brisk return fire and Major Samuel Harries of Trevacoon refused categorically to hand out any ransom money'.[60] He gives no source for this statement. Two days after the invasion, Vaughan tried again. He wrote to Portland:

> I beg leave to remark to your Grace that had these ships [the French] moored in Fishguard Bay both the Fort and Town of Fishguard would have been battered to pieces. I having but three pounds of Ammunition for my Guns [being Eight Nine pounders] to oppose to them. I therefore hope your Grace will judge it proper to order me some Powder for this service as soon as Possible this fort being very defenceless for want of it I have some time [since] made a report to the Board of Ordnance what stores I have.[61]

He might have added that in any case, the choice of anchorage by the French made them safe from any danger from the guns of the fort.

And so what of the appearance of the town? Fishguard at the time was like many of the towns in west Wales. It was what contemporaries would have called it, and indeed did describe it as, a wretched town. In 1795 it was reported that: 'Fishguard in the aggregate looks well, and conveys to you the idea of a large flourishing place' but, 'we say "from Fishguard streets and Cardigan streets Good Lord deliver us"'.[62] Another visitor in 1803 said of Fishguard that the whitewash of the roofs gave the town a clean appearance 'which is contrasted by rugged dirty streets with a dung-heap at almost every door'.[63] Nevertheless, it seems to have been an important port, exporting corn – often controversially, sea produce, and other goods.

As to the government of the town and district, and the treatment of the poor, in 1795 a visitor wrote that:

> The price of labour here bears no proportion to the advance which all the necessaries of life have of late experienced Parochial business is managed here in a very slovenly manner by a junto, who claim a sort of hereditary right to lead the parish by the nose, a set of people, insolent and arbitrary like all usurpers, yet in whose assumed authority, and unresisted decisions, the herd, who are either too ignorant or too indolent to put things on a better footing, tamely acquiesce.

He goes on to describe how the poor from the district 'instigated by actual want, and the unsatisfied clamours of their children and families, met to remonstrate in the most moving and peaceable manner' against the export of a cargo of corn and butter. They were met with charges of riot, and the magistrates accused by such 'harpies' of being too lenient.[64] 'A committee of vestry', had been appointed to 'thoroughly clean this Augean stable'. But the writer has little hope except for the exertions of Mr Knox, whose family, as we have begun to see, forms an important part of this story.

And of the people? Again, Gwinfardd Dyfed writing in 1795, claims that, 'There are few districts in the whole principality where there are no manufactures more populous than this, and none in which there is less provision for rendering the population useful'. He estimates the population in the town at about 2,000, and in other parts of the parish at 800.[65] We have noted that it was commonplace for visitors to lament the lack of imagination when it came to mining, industry, agriculture and indeed every activity upon which livelihood depended. The Fishguard district was no exception. Thus, as we have noted, the same writer in 1795 deplored the indifference of local people to the improvement of their fisheries writing that they would not start to fish until 'the fish almost leap into the houses which skirt the tide'. Their attitude was rigid even though the catches were getting smaller, and together with potatoes 'constitutes the principal food of the lower orders'.[66]

But in the light of an imminent invasion, what about their capacity to fight? That very eminent son of Pembrokeshire, Richard Fenton, had some harsh words to say about his fellow countymen:

> Mean and simple, short of growth, broad and shrubby [sic], unacceptable in fight for the most part, however they prove in action when they are put to it … so that of all the countries [sic] of Wales I am bold to pronounce (and I speak by experience) Pembrokeshire to be the worst of manred [sic] and hardest to find serviceable men, so that the lieutenants and commissioners for muster, are more toiled in seeking 50 personable men, than their neighbours are to find 100.[67]

Thus it can be seen that the lives of the peasantry of west Wales at the time of the invasion were in general characterised by poverty, starvation, and that hopelessness which was described by a Pembrokeshire priest as long before as 1721 as, 'the marks of a forsaken poverty and desolation which seem to overspread the whole neighbourhood'.[68] Another much later priest, in this case Basil Jones, the bishop of St David's from 1874 until 1896, went further perhaps by saying that 'St. David's is about the largest and poorest of all the dioceses in this realm'.[69] And this was 150 years after Saunders wrote. It is important to emphasise that throughout the eighteenth and nineteenth centuries the misery of the people of Pembrokeshire was not sporadic, or periodic, but chronic, persisting, and crushing.

Pembrokeshire then was a world of exceptional wealth and miserable deprivation. It would appear to be a place exactly suited to the assumptions underlying the instructions given by the French General Hoche to Tate, the commanding officer of the invasion force:

> In all countries the poor are the class most prone to insurrection, and this disposition is to be forwarded by distributing money and drink, by inveighing against the government as the cause of public distress, by recommending and facilitating a rising to plunder the public stores and magazines and the property of The rich, whose affluence is the natural subject of envy to the poor.

We now go on to try to understand why the French wanted to invade such a poor place at all.

France, the Revolution, and the Context of the Invasion

Two of the most important world events in the later eighteenth century were the revolutions in America and France. There were significant links between the two. For example, the French supported the Americans in their struggle, and the experience of the Americans was invaluable to the French in theirs. A commonly expressed view is that the involvement of the French in America caused many French people to question the way in which their country was governed, and was therefore an important stimulus to the revolutionary movement. The American war was deeply unpopular amongst intellectual people in Britain, and below we review the considerable influence wielded by one of the opponents, the Welsh Unitarian minister Richard Price. When the French revolution began in 1789, it was hailed as an example of how tyrannical regimes throughout Europe could be overthrown. Such views were held by public figures such as William Wordsworth, and Richard Sheridan. When war broke out between Britain and France, there was considerable opposition to it, and later some of that opposition by Welsh writers shall be reviewed.

There was one aspect of the policies emanating from France which should be dwelt upon, as it was central to the Welsh attitude to the revolution. A central plank of those policies was the destruction of the power of the Roman Catholic Church, which comprised the First Estate in the French system and under the *ancien régime* had been the biggest landholder in France. In December 1789, February 1790, and July 1790, laws were passed which took over Church property, ended monastic vows, ended a levy on crops called the *dime*, and made clergy employees of the state. The *dime* is rather reminiscent of the tithe system which was to create such anger, and ultimately violence in nineteenth-century Wales.

The collective Welsh attitude to these anti-Church moves in revolutionary France was of unadulterated joy. The lower classes in Wales were largely nonconformists, and the people whose writings have survived, approving of the revolution were, in the main, nonconformist ministers. The nonconformists suffered discrimination because of their faith; were violently opposed to the Established Church of England; and entertained what can only be described as a pathological hatred of Rome. Some believed that the Reformation was unfinished and that its ideals had been betrayed. If such statements seem excessive, the justice in making them can be seen by reference to one, not exceptional, set of statements by a prominent figure, Morgan John Rhys.

In 1793 he published in his magazine a summary of a book written in English by James Bicheno. The rather wordy title was: 'The signs of the Times' or the overthrow of Papal Tyranny in France, the Prelude of Destruction to Popery and Despotism, but of Peace to Mankind.' In this work, 'the French Revolution was portrayed as the work of God. Its purpose was to undermine Christian corruptions generally and Popery in particular'.[1] Rhys translated the work into Welsh so swiftly that Welsh readers had access to it before a review appeared in an English journal. It seeks to compare the events of the revolution with the Book of Revelation. In this odd work, which is very much located in its time, the 'fall of the tenth part of the city, the French Revolution, was not the end of God's retributive justice; other anti Christian institutions, and in particular the Papacy would perish':[2] while 'The Jacobins were God's agents in so far as they were the opponents of Popish despotism'.[3]

Unfortunately for extremist nonconformist opinion, the hope of the death of Catholicism in France was not to be realised. Despite the legislation, and the imprisonment and slaughter of priests, by the turn of the century and the rise of Napoleon, who had different priorities, the latter realised that some accommodation with the Catholic Church had to be achieved. In 1801 he arrived at a Concordat which brought about a new relationship between Church and State.

What is the relevance of either the American or the French revolutions to life in Pembrokeshire at the time of the invasion? Can the claims of writers such as Gwyn A. Williams be justified, as in his attempt to link the two revolutions?

The American example, charged now with French styles, drenched every radical and protest movement in the turbulent Wales of the 1790s – in books, leaflets, journals, and graffiti ... from the 1790s the number of political texts in Welsh had multiplied six-fold.[4]

To understand much of the course of events and especially the aftermath, it is appropriate at this point to discuss what knowledge local people might have had about these events, their ability to discover information, and the sources from whence such information might have come.

The first difficulty, which is generic in historical deduction, is that the voice of poor people is seldom recorded. To take the example of the invasion, we have a detailed account by Thomas Knox of events as he perceived them to be. It should be said that, even though the purpose of his account is to defend himself, it is an accurate version. We also have the account by the Duke of Rutland in which he sets down what Lord Cawdor told him. We have some official reports and correspondence, which have a specific purpose, to put the best possible construction on the affair. There is a wealth of literature which *purports* to report what ordinary people said or did. But we shall go on to see that the reliability of such oral evidence is questionable: a fact which is compounded by the distance in time between the invasion, and much of the writing on it. The brief extract (set out in a later chapter), from the letter by Griffith, one of the defendants in the treason trials, is rare indeed as an expression of experience by a humbler member of the community. The basic fact is that the views of powerless people were made clear mostly in social disorder.

So did major outside events have any impact on a county which was so remote, and large numbers of whose population were unable to speak or read English? The first point to be considered is the ability or inability of people to read and write. Although formal schooling at the end of the eighteenth century was sparse, Wales generally had a tradition of reading from the seventeenth century onwards. Geraint Evans is one who draws attention to the level of literacy in Wales by the seventeenth century by reference to the fact that yeoman farmers and tradesmen and others 'of middling sorts' had 'a growing appetite for pious literature'.[5] In the eighteenth century books such as *Canwyll y Camry* (The Welshman's Candle) were widely dispensed by charitable bodies who published 'sizeable editions at cheap rates and distributed many of them free of charge to the deserving poor.'[6] When it comes to literacy, there was notable, not to say remarkable, teaching activity, especially in Pembrokeshire.

The most famous example is Griffith Jones (b.1683) of Llanddowror, which is situated on the road between Carmarthen and Tenby. Jones pioneered what came to be known as Circulating Schools.

This system involved the selection and training of teachers who then travelled around the countryside, and through the medium of the Bible taught both adults and children to read Welsh. In the case of non-speaking south Pembrokeshire they were taught in English: this was the system of 'Circulating Schools'. Much has been written about the scale of Jones' operation until his death in 1761. And although there has been much discussion about the numbers of schools and the number of pupils, the calculations do not differ in any significant way. Jones himself claimed that he set up 3,495 schools, in which 158,237 pupils had been taught: this total did not include adults. Glanmor Williams, in a modern count, does not differ much: 'the true totals would seem to have been 3325 schools in just under 1600 places with 153,835 pupils'.[7] Most other estimates are within this range. Then there was the effort made to teach adults. Williams believes that Jones' claim that for every child two adults attended classes is 'too generous a proportion'. He supports 'the most recent critical estimates of recent years', which is 200,000. Bearing in mind that the estimated population of Wales in the period of his life was between 400,000 and 500,000, and that his efforts were focussed upon west Wales, it has to be agreed that this was a remarkable achievement, which must have led to a high level of intellectual enquiry on the part of substantial numbers of people.

Although the primary aim was to teach literacy so that the students could read religious material, it is a commonplace of educational experience that, once people are possessed of literacy skills, these cannot be confined to some limited, specific end. It follows that the attention of those who could read would turn to secular literature, especially the literature which was spawned by the two revolutions. This literature, it should be noted at once, was published in both English and Welsh. And there was plenty of printed material available. The first printing press in Wales was set up by Isaac Carter in 1718 near Newcastle Emlyn, which is not very far from Fishguard, and it was a Welsh text which was the first book to be printed in Carmarthen in 1723.[8]

There was a rich literature of writing about the revolutions, and Welshmen were very much in the forefront of this. The most prominent was the Glamorganshire Unitarian minister, Richard Price (1723–1791).

His distinction in his lifetime was considerable. The detail of his work need not be set out here, but a few examples will serve to illustrate the point. He wrote texts which were extremely important, on economic and financial affairs. When America became independent, prominent members in the new government 'were specially deputed by Congress to invite Dr. Price to give his assistance in regulating the finances of the New Republic'.[9] Amongst his many political works was *Observations in the Nature of Civil Liberty, The Principles of Government and the Justice and Policy of the War with America*. 1000 copies were sold in two days, and 60,000 in six months. The work was translated into German, French and Dutch, and of course published in America. He was given the Freedom of the City of London, was awarded an honorary degree from Yale university (the only other recipient was George Washington), and he was offered, but turned down, an invitation to become an American citizen. In 1789 he published *A discourse on the love of our country* in which he hailed the revolution just beginning in France:

> Be encouraged, all ye friends of freedom and writers in its defence! The times are auspicious. Your labours have not been in vain. Behold kingdoms, admonished by you, starting from sleep, breaking their fetters, and claiming justice from their oppressors! Behold the light you have struck out, after setting AMERICA free, reflected to France, and there kindled into a flame that lays despotism in ashes, and warms and illuminates EUROPE![10]

The depth of Price's feelings may be judged from a speech he gave on 14 July in London to celebrate the first anniversary of the Revolution. He proposed a toast: 'An Alliance between Great Britain and France for perpetuating peace, and making the whole world free and happy.' His speech was so well received that it was sent to France and read twice in the National Assembly, all the members having removed their hats. The commitment to revolutionary, democratic ideals is summed up in this statement: 'I am grateful to heaven' [Price said] 'for having extended my life, so that, after sharing the benefit of one revolution, I have been spared to be a witness of two other revolutions, both glorious.'[11]

He did not live to see the French revolution run its course (he died in 1791), and it is to be wondered if he would have become disillusioned at what happened when the notion of spreading revolution turned to imperial aggrandisement. Indeed it is to be wondered what he might have thought of his perceived perfect states as, seemingly inevitably, they became corrupted. The fact of this corruption does not diminish the enormous impact of his writing; writing which is still not sufficiently recognised for its influence.

A discourse on the love of our country created a most significant development in the ideological writing about the French revolution. Edmund Burke was so incensed by it, that he published his *Reflections on the French Revolution* (1790). Even more significant was the fact that Thomas Paine, in turn, was prompted to reply to Burke with the classic *The Rights of Man*. The essence of the latter was soon to be made available *in Welsh*, for those who could not manage the English version. This created some alarm as can be seen from a letter from a spy in Cardiff to the Home Office that, 'It is known to be a certainty that a Welchman of great talents is translating Tom Paine's book in Welch & doing great mischief thro' the strong espousal he has given the French cause.'[12] A spy in north Wales wrote to the Home Office on 19 December 1792 about the danger of, 'Infusing into their minds the pernicious tenets of Paine's 'Rights of Man', upon whose book, I am told, public lectures are delivered to a considerable number in the neighbourhood of Wrexham, by a Methodist. The pernicious effects of them are too evident in that parish.'[13]

The likely candidate for the title of this 'Welchman of great talents' was John Jones, best known by his Welsh *nom de plume* Jac Glan-y-gors. Jones (1766–1821), who was a native of Denbighshire, wrote two Welsh volumes which are generally supposed to embrace the ideas of Tom Paine. They were *Seren Tan Gwmmwl* (A star under a cloud), published in 1795, and *Toriad y Dydd* (Daybreak), published in 1797, the very year of the Pembrokeshire invasion. Glan-y-gors was, after Price, the most unrelenting critic of the state of British society and of monarchy, which seemed to him to be the quintessence of all that was wrong. With his background it is not surprising that he drew upon biblical analogy in expressing 'surprise at the blindness of the Israelites of old, in persisting in having a king'. His sense of humour, always present in his writing, is demonstrated in his comment on the appointment of William and Mary who 'neither of them knew more about the laws and regulations of the kingdom, than a mole knows about the sun'. Bishops too were castigated by him. They were 'greater oppressors of their parishioners than ever Nero was at Rome'. The money paid to them 'would do far more good in teaching the poor children of Wales, who were then kept in a cloud of ignorance'. And of course he praised America, 'the morning star of liberty'.[14]

There were other Welsh writers who not only supported, but influenced the course of the American and French revolutions. David Williams (1738–1816) was described by Brissot de Warville, a major figure in the French revolution, as 'one of the foremost political thinkers in England, and the least tainted with national prejudices, as he had embraced the cause of humanity'.[15] When it was decided to offer French citizenship to a number of foreigners, Williams was one to whom the offer was made. This came as no surprise, since he had written of the revolution that it was 'an event the most beneficial to humanity in all the records of mankind'.[16] Another radical writer was Thomas Evans, also known as Tomos Glyn Cothi (1764–1833). A pioneer of the doctrine of Unitarianism in Wales, he was imprisoned and put in the pillory in Carmarthen in 1801 for allegedly singing a seditious song, the *Carmagnol*, which contained the lines:

> The thundering guns of France shall roar,
> Vile George shall trembling stand
> Or flee his native land,
> With terror and appall

As well as this, Tomos edited the first issue of *Y Drysorfa Gymmysgedig* (The Welsh Repository) in 1795. In this first issue, there is a 'Hymn to be sung on the Fast Day', which speaks of 'the rapacious spoilers that waded in blood' and the hope that God would 'hurl headlong from their high seats, in one brief hour, those world-oppressors; and scatter the people who had fattened on human blood'.[17] This was typical of those publications which 'provided space for other writers, to present their views to the monoglot Welshman'.[18]

Another Welsh writer who was highly regarded in France was Morgan John Rhys (1760–1804). For him the revolution, 'had opened an important door for the preaching of the Gospel, and the circulation of the scriptures in France'.[19] In his writing he attacked those who waged war against France, claiming, in a sermon of February 1794, that 'those who fought against France were also fighting against religious and civil liberty, and were fighting for the cause of Tyranny and Popery'.[20] The previous year, he reminded people how Prime Minister Pitt had been declared, 'an enemy of the human race' by the French government.[21] Many such writers saw America as the land of religious freedom. Rhys saw America as, 'A new State, in which "dwelleth righteousness" established by God on earth-a country, bestowing privileges upon its cities, in the enjoyment of as good a government as was ever instituted upon the earth.'[22] Eventually Rhys went to America, in part to escape from the British government, and set up a colony called Beulah, which attracted a good deal of attention. He also changed his name to Rhees.[23]

A somewhat remarkable figure is generally included amongst those who wrote supporting the French Revolution. This is Edward Williams-Iolo Morganwg, (1747–1826), who described himself as 'The bard of Liberty'. He was, it is claimed, in contact with many of the leaders including Talleyrand, Franklin, Priestley and Paine.[24] He wrote about Liberty in a song, which has been claimed as in parallel with Paine's *The Rights of Man*,[25] surely an extravagant claim. Amongst his less revolutionary ideas was the resurrection of the mythology of much 'Welsh culture', especially druidism. Much of this was fraudulent, such as when he 'discovered' and published the work of Welsh poets, which in fact he had fabricated. His bizarre behaviour may be in part to a lifelong addiction to laudanum. Nevertheless, he has a place, however odd, in the Welsh literary scene at the end of the eighteenth century.

There are two further observations to be made about Welsh writing at the end of the eighteenth century. The first is that not all the well-known writers were for revolution, or even the encouragement of protest. Typical of the more conservative writers was David Thomas (Dafydd Ddu o Eryri) (1759–1822), of whom a later commentator wrote that 'his delight was in rule and law: contentment, to his mind, was the duty and happiness of subjects.'[26] It was alleged that he even, perhaps humorously, 'never missed an opportunity to sing when anything occurred in connection with the royal family-such as a birth, marriage, restoration to health, death etc.'[27] In any case, there was on the part of many Welsh writers, 'sickly repetition of the fawning flattery, that was never wanting on the lips of the great majority of the bards of the time, to the House of Brunswick in general, and the then King George in particular.'[28]

The eminent Rev. Thomas Charles of Bala was one of many who felt that Methodists had to be defended against the charge of disloyalty. In November 1799, he wrote a reply to such an allegation that appeared in *The Gentlemen's Magazine*: 'Can any fact speak more avowedly, and more forcibly in proof of the loyalty of Welsh Methodists, than that, on the Anniversary of the reduction of the French invaders in South Wales, the Methodists have a public day of thanksgiving for that mercy?'[29] Some establishment groups seem to have been ambivalent. Even the London Welsh society Gwyneddigion, which was hardly radical, announced that at the 1790 Eisteddfod in St Asaph, literary prizes - a silver chair and a silver medal - would be offered for works on:

> *Liberty.* The most precious treasure on the face of the earth, for out of it emanates, and upon it are pillowed, most of human happiness this side of the grave. Liberty curbs violence, rends the snares of False Philanthropy, and Superstition, which oppress and enslave all the good qualities which belong to man's nature ... in its defence, our ancestors struggled with splendid courage for centuries.[30]

It was a curiosity, then, that the first prize went to Dafydd Ddo Eryri, an arch conservative for his ode .'There is nothing to indicate sympathy with, or indeed knowledge of the French Revolution'. Equally strange was the award of the second prize to Gwallter Mechain, whose political views were the same, although he referred slightly to events in France, such as the fall of the Bastille. Davies' view is that, 'to the Gwyneddigion Society, who gave the prize, both odes must have been a great disappointment'.[31]

The second point is that as the revolution in France changed its several courses; due to the execution of the king; and then because of the Terror; and then as a result of the expansionist policies of Napoleon; the sympathies of some of the more admiring writers began to wane. This may have been genuine, or it may have been prompted by increasing persecution by the British government. Even so stern a critic of the British government as Morgan John Rhys, 'strongly protested that he was loyal to the British Government; and in the second number of *Y Cylch-grawn* he expresses his fervent wish that Providence might keep the family of Hanover on the throne.'[32]

In addition to the ideologically serious outpourings of these writers, there was in circulation a huge amount of ballads, broadsides, chap books, story books, and newspapers. It will be remembered that after the riot by Hook miners in Haverfordwest, the magistrate suggested that notices of rewards should be put into newspapers which were widely read in Pembrokeshire at the time.

So there was a huge variety of material available to keep the substantial proportion of Welsh people who were literate, and even those who were not, informed about events of the day, and *the* event of the day was the French revolution, and the war with France. Awareness of this welter of debate, and its accompanying literature, helps to understand the seemingly mysterious, and commonly agreed injustice, of the trial of local farmers for treason after the invasion.

Another singularly Welsh source of information was the accumulated knowledge of the drovers. In this respect, these were as important in Pembrokeshire as anywhere in Wales, since the Pembrokeshire Castlemartin breed of cattle were amongst the most popular in the English markets. Colyer makes a very strong case for the drovers as transmitters of culture, and above all, information. He also emphasises the fact that although he had his social critics –'the drover was sometimes a rough customer'[33] –, there were amongst them cultivated, civilised and wealthy men:

> A great deal has been written about the contribution of the drovers to the cultural and social life of Wales. This is rightly so, especially before the nineteenth century when mobility was restricted and a relatively small proportion of the working population had the opportunity of travelling far beyond their home villages. The drovers enjoyed the advantages of extensive contact with English culture, social life, farming systems and financial matters, besides representing an essential communications link with England.[34]

Nowhere was this more the case than in Pembrokeshire.

A critical question which must arise is whether ordinary people in a county as remote as Pembrokeshire could have been aware of this literature, and the activities concomitant with it. Because of sympathy, especially in the early stages, with the Revolution, various societies were established, which were to cause the British government considerable concern. Perhaps the most prominent of these was the London Corresponding Society which came into being in 1792. There is some evidence that its influence reached into Wales. In December 1793 a committee meeting of the Society recorded that a letter from Wales was read, and a John Jones who lived near Bala 'had resolutions of the Society printed in Welsh'.[35]

So did all these movements and ideas have any impact in such an isolated county as Pembrokeshire? In the absence of very firm evidence, it has been claimed that they did not. But there are historians who insist that this volume of literature must have been read by someone, and indeed that the political causes in it were regarded with interest and sympathy. Gwyn A. Williams is one who is adamant about the spirit of revolution arising from the despair of the poorer people. Taking the case of Richard Price, he writes that Price's kinsfolk were 'radical colonisers of the Welsh mind', and that 'David Jones, the Welsh Freeholder, preached the doctrines of the Unitarian democrat Dr. Joseph Priestley as a way of life'.[36] Specifically of south-west Wales, he claims that even as late as the 1830s and 1840s the region was:

> In quasi permanent crisis ... Cardiganshire was the most disturbed ... county in Wales ... the Galicia of Wales ... Carmarthenshire [was in] a kind of secession from public order ... there was a rooted populist radicalism in Carmarthen, fed by its neighbour village, which could make it a 'sans-culotte' sort of place.[37]

He goes on to insist that the 'related notions of isolation, backwardness and "primitive rivals"' should be dismissed. Instead he insists 'that complex in south Cardiganshire/north Carmarthenshire/north Pembrokeshire ... was the human matrix of so many working-class movements'.[38]

After the surrender, it was reported to the Duke of Rutland that Pembrokeshire people were notably 'disloyal', which is to say that their allegiance may have been in doubt, bold assertions that shall be discussed later. It was certainly the case, as we shall go on to see, that a number of local men were charged with treason. The Pembrokeshire historian Fenton, although distrusting of the evidence against them, still regarded the defendants as, 'an ignorant fanatic or two of the Baptist sect ... poisoned, as by all accounts they were, by the seditious publications of that time.'[39]

The huge power of the French Revolution was, manifestly widespread. At the end of the eighteenth century, Davies and Edwards wrote: 'though Wales still remained more backward than England, the spirit of change was abroad, the old established order began to break up, and even in remote places the fiery breath of the French Revolution seared, or quickened, men's minds, according to their interpretation of it.'[40]

In 1797, the year of the invasion of Pembrokeshire, the French revolution was still in a state of turmoil. Several forms of government had been advocated and tried. In September 1792 the monarchy was abolished, and the republic established. A few months later, in January 1793 King Louis XVI was executed, to be followed by the Queen, Marie Antoinette, nine months later. For a variety of reasons – French defeats on the battlefields; pressure from the *sans-culottes* (a mixed group including the poor, radicals, workers, craftsmen, and small traders); and consequent radical laws – the serious unrest and attempts at counter revolution were contained by the exercise of that famous repression from 5 September 1793 to 27 July 1794, which is known as the Reign of Terror. But now Robespierre, its most frightening physical manifestation, had been overthrown and executed; and France, though able to feel some sense of relief, had still to live with an uncertain future.

After The Terror came government by the Directory: 'The Directory was unpopular at home, being widely regarded as bureaucratic, corrupt and oppressive, while abroad the armies won famous victories and encapsulated everything that was most glorious and patriotic in the revolutionary dream.'[41]

We shall go on to see that an important strategic aim of this government came to be the invasion of Ireland, of which the invasion of Pembrokeshire was a sort of offshoot. But these attacks, not least that on Pembrokeshire, were sometimes attended by bad luck, notably terrible weather, but more usually by half-hearted commitment, indecision, personal squabbles, and indifferent organisation. Some reported that this was a hallmark of the way in which the Directory operated:

> It was Sandoz [the Prussian ambassador] who summarized for Frederick William the confusion at the centre which consistently blurred the Directory's strategic aims: 'I hear politics is managed now as finance', he wrote in June 1797, 'from day to day, and from event to event … When I wanted to know the state of the present negotiations with Austria … I could verify that no member of the Executive Directory knew exactly of what they consisted'.[42]

An important feature of the several revolutionary regimes was the shake up in the army which enabled the promotion of those who had ability, regardless of the humble nature of their origins:

The revolutionaries found new officers from within the ranks of the army itself, from the many corporals and sergeants who had distinguished themselves in the wars of the late eighteenth century but who could have nurtured no thoughts of promotion in the royal regiments. Promotion was now based on talent, not on birth.[43]

Aside from the stunning example of Napoleon:

A galaxy of unknown men were suddenly propelled to the forefront of the army, which they were called upon to lead after very little experience, and at a comparatively young age … Bernadotte, who enlisted at the age of seventeen, rose from the rank of sergeant to become a general in four years. In 1796, Lannier, an ostler's son was *chef de brigade* at the age of twenty seven.[44]

One of these military stars was Louis Lazare Hoche, son of a worker in the royal stables. Born in 1768, he soon distinguished himself in the revolutionary army. And he was the victor in the Quiberon landing in 1795, when the British were cut off; a victory which was to have such resonance in the invasion of Pembrokeshire. By the age of twenty-five Hoche was a general. But despite his considerable success (for example in 1793 he pushed the Austro-Prussian armies out of Alsace), he was not immune (nobody was), to the venom of the Committee of Public Safety. In March 1794, having been accused by rival Charles Picnegru, Hoche was arrested as a traitor and imprisoned. He was one of the lucky people who were released when the regime came to an end in July 1794. In the light of his subsequent career, it was fortunate for his country too. His death in September 1797 at the age of twenty-nine also affected the course of French history, for he may well have stopped Napoleon's rise to power. His admirer and colleague, Wolfe Tone, was extremely upset at his death, and wrote to his wife: 'I know not what I may do, myself on this occasion, nor shall I for a few days-adieu, dearest Life; I am in very severe affliction.'[45]

By the time the Directory was at work, Hoche was held in high regard. The genesis of the plans to invade Britain began with his rapid promotion to General. Lazare Carnot, the member responsible for the army wrote to him that:

No one can instil such fear into the English or deal the fatal blow better than the man who crushed the cancer of the Vendee and the Chouans; I am

convinced that your name alone will double our strength in enemy eyes,
intensify their terror and increase the confidence of the Irish who want to
break the yoke of their oppressors.[46]

This was a reference to one of his most important achievements; the significant and vital defeat of a British inspired attack by royalists and émigrés at Quiberon in 1795, when vast quantities of British material were captured. One of the oddities of this was the fact that included in the booty were British uniforms, and in the event these were dyed in dark colours, and were used to clothe the soldiers who were to invade Pembrokeshire. It was on this account that the force was called the *Legion Noire*.

A very critical meeting took place in July 1795 between Hoche, who was anxious to punish Britain for its part in the insurrections in France, and Wolfe Tone, 'The prophet of Irish independence'.[47] Tone was then aged thirty-two, and his 'negotiations in Paris helped shape France's Irish policy for many years to come'.[48] He asked for a commission in the French army, saying that he did not want to be hanged as a traitor if he were to be captured. He was made a *chef de brigade* (roughly approximating to colonel).[49] But in the event such a precaution did not save him. When he was eventually captured in Ireland, he was sentenced as a traitor to be hanged.

This person of such influence in the ruling circles in France was utterly convinced that an invasion of Ireland would be a success. It also happened that he and Hoche liked each other, both personally and because they shared many of the same views. Tone convinced Hoche to accept the idea, and in December 1796 a French fleet set sail for Ireland, with Hoche on board. But a combination of bad weather and some skill on the part of the British navy led to disaster for the French.[50]

But Tone remained resolute, and now drew attention to what he saw as the opportunities presented by the naval mutinies in 1797, in the Nore and at Spithead. His interest was fired by two facts. The British fleet was very powerful, and posed a real hindrance to any invasion plans, and so the possibility of the fleet being disabled was very important. Secondly, the large number of Irishmen who were serving in the British navy which Tone saw an important factor. One estimate is that there were 100,000 seamen, and 20,000 marines, which figure included officers. Of these seamen some 11,500 were Irish, and about 4,000 were marines.[51] Tone however, with his chronic tendency towards optimism and exaggeration, stated that there were 80,000 Irishmen in the navy.[52]

Although it is not clear how many belonged to the Society of the United Irish, the radical group of which Tone had been one of the members, Tone believed that Irish nationality was enough. Pursuing his belief in the patriotic fervour of his fellow countrymen, Tone took it upon himself to send a stirring exhortation, probably disseminated in 1796, to revolt. In this he stated that:

> Ireland is now at war with England in defence of her liberties; France is the ally of Ireland, and England is the common enemy of both nations. You are aboard the British navy. You will probably be called upon immediately to turn your arms against your native land I hope and rely that you will act as becomes brave Seamen and honest Irishmen.

He goes on to encourage the seamen to seize their ships and sail them into Irish ports. If they did so, the ships and contents would be sold, and the profits distributed. Those who did not want to go to sea again would be allowed to go home. The officers would be powerless: 'depend upon it, they dare not stir, if they you once resolved'.[53]

But as often happened there was a curious inertia about much of the behaviour of the French government. Leaving aside the difficult question as to how realistic it was to coordinate a rising, while there were reserves of British troops in readiness to prevent any such happening, an invasion would have had to be attempted soon, and that was not the style of the French at this time. Naturally, 'Tone looked back on the lost opportunity with bitter feelings':

> Damn it, damn it, damn it! … there seems to be a fate in This business. Five weeks, I believe six weeks, the English fleet Was paralysed by the mutinies at Portsmouth, Plymouth and the Nore. The sea was open, and nothing to prevent both the French Fleets to put to sea. Well nothing was ready; that precious opportunity, which we can never expect to return was lost.[54]

The French people by this time were desirous of peace. But there was one exception; Britain: 'Anglophobia, nurtured on years of propaganda, which had erroneously attributed the Revolution's difficulties to English espionage and "Pitt's gold". In the government, only perhaps Talleyrand did not share this hatred of England.'[55]

By 1796 The Directory had formed a resolve to attack Ireland, and in June wrote to Hoche with an ambitious plan:

> We intend, Citizen General, to restore to a people ripe for revolution the independence and liberty for which it clamours. Ireland has groaned under the hated English yoke for centuries ... detach Ireland from England, and she will be reduced to a second-rate power and deprived of most of her superiority over the seas.[56]

But Elliott's verdict is that this was 'an-ill-thought out scheme (which) was to undergo considerable modification in the course of the summer'.[57] Certainly there was chronic uncertainty and disagreement amongst the most senior of the officers. Admiral Villaret Joyeuse was not a supporter of the idea of invading Ireland, and in the event was replaced and accused by Hoche of crucial delays in getting the fleet to sea. On 16 December 1796, the expedition finally left Brest. It consisted of seventeen ships of the line, together with support vessels, and some 15,000 of the best soldiers in the French army, with guns and ammunition for the rebels in Ireland, who it was supposed, would turn out to meet, and join them.

Nervous of meeting a superior British force, there was uncertainty about the best course to take, and this was compounded by atrocious weather, which resulted in the fleet being divided. Eventually most of the fleet met in Bantry Bay on 29 December. There was no improvement in the weather, and there was in any case no mobilisation of local people, and Hoche was a very long way from the main force, which in itself brought two disadvantages. Firstly he had kept his plans secret, and so his staff did not learn until quite late what they were supposed to be doing, and secondly he could take no significant part in what was fast becoming an impossible situation. By the end of the month it was agreed that the operation should be abandoned, and there should be a return to Brest. 'Eleven vessels and some 5000 men had been lost, as well as all the returned ships being damaged'.[58] As often happened, in the words of the wit Sydney Smith: 'The winds – those ancient and unsubsidised allies of England – the winds, upon which ministers depend for saving kingdoms as washerwomen do for drying clothes.'[59] The attempt to foment a rising in Ireland had been a total failure.

Carnot, who was to be famed for his military genius also devised a plan to send a smaller force to England. He set out his plan, which does not accord with his generally agreed record of brilliance and seems to be both idealistic, and in the light of subsequent events, absurd:

> The men employed in this expedition ought to be, as far as possible, young, robust and daring, with minds open to the allure of booty ... they should know how to carry terror and death into the midst of their enemies ... in these troops might be incorporated men sentenced to prison or the galleys, if they are known to have the physical and moral qualities necessary. They should be assured that they will be allowed to keep whatever booty they acquire, and to enjoy quiet possession of it in some of our colonies ... no large provision of stores and clothing will be needed: the resources of the legion will be its courage and arms ... on arrival the chiefs should proclaim themselves to be *avengers of liberty* and *enemies of tyrants* ... They must swear *war to the mansion* and *peace to the cottage*, and their conduct, especially at first should conform to their declaration.[60]

So there were other plans to invade Britain, most designed to create diversion, and to draw the British navy away from Ireland. Cornwall and Wales were to be targeted, but the Cornish venture was dropped, and instead it was proposed to attack the north-east of England where they would set about destroying coalmines and shipping, and then march to Lancashire. Somehow they would then meet the other force which would come up through Wales. For the purpose of the invasion of the north-east flat-bottomed boats were built. These appeared to be so risky that the officers, led by General Quantin, had serious reservations, as did their force of convicts and deserters, which was dignified by the name of the *Legion Franche.* When they were persuaded to sail, the boats proved un-seaworthy, and the expedition made an ignominious return to Dunkirk. The third invasion, that of Pembrokeshire, will be dealt with later.

Eventually Wolfe's dream was realised, if only to the extent that there *were* some minor invasions of Ireland after the rebellion broke out in that country in 1798. The first of these was the most successful of all, at least in the short term, for in this attack General Humbert landed a force of some 11,000 men in County Mayo in 1798. He had set out with some 4,000, but many were delayed and ran into British ships. Despite this, the invaders penetrated some way inland before they were finally over-come. They defeated a much bigger force at the Races of Castlebar, and advanced to within some eighty miles of Dublin. But eventually they had to surrender. Tone's brother, Matthew, was one of those captured, and he was tried and hanged. The second invasion achieved nothing.

In the third of these, Wolfe took part, and was on board the warship *Hoche* when she was taken by the English squadron. He was duly tried, and asked that as he was a French officer, he should be shot rather than hanged. His request was denied and he was sentenced to be hanged on November 12 1798. In prison he managed to cut his throat, and died a few days later. He was thirty-five, and is generally regarded as the father of the Irish battle for independence.

The officer chosen to lead the earlier invasion force, the one which finally landed in Pembrokeshire, was William Tate. He was given the rank of *chef de brigade*, which, as has been pointed out, roughly equated to the rank of colonel. One of A.L. Williams' historical careless inaccuracies, is that he raises him to the rank of general.[61] Tate was a strange choice. He was not French, could not speak French, was an American, and was, it is generally agreed, some seventy years old. It is often supposed that one reason for choosing him was that since English was his mother tongue, he would be able to communicate with the local people whose support was assumed. Since the first language of the people of north Pembrokeshire was Welsh, this is one of the many mysteries surrounding the expedition. It may, of course simply be the case that the planners did not know of the Welsh language.

Tate was a commissioned officer in the War of American Independence, and was taken prisoner in 1780: 'Many years afterwards in Paris, no less a person than James Monroe was to testify that Tate had served with the marked approbation of General Washington and his officers.' Jones deploys a caveat, that Tate was brought before a military court in 1780 on a charge of making improper returns, and reprimanded.[62] It has also been suggested by a French biographer of Hoche, that Tate's family were murdered by Indians who had sided with Britain in the War, and that this added to his virulent hatred of the British.[63] Tate's career in the early 1790s included a period of involvement with Edmond Genet, French Minister Plenipotentiary to the United States, in the attempt to drive the Spanish out of Louisiana and the Floridas. The failure of these plans, together with the concomitant personal losses, and danger to himself, led him to seek refuge in France, arriving there in 1795.

Fulsome praise of Tate's conduct came from the French consul in Charleston. In his opinion Tate had:

All the virtues of the adventurers who conquered the two Indies, without
their vices and ignorance; extremely severe to himself, drinking nothing but
water; a firm disciplinarian and having in his brain the coolness and the heat
necessary to execute a great enterprise with small means. He conceives in the
minute, decides on the instant; he carves on the right joint.[64]

During his stay in France he proposed several ambitious schemes, such as
an expedition to capture Jamaica. Such schemes, as well as some of those
he advanced in the United States led Stuart Jones to sum him up as having
'had a fertile brain and was full of wild schemes of one kind or another'.[65]
It may be fairly claimed though that all of the evidence from his earlier
career, before he went to France, marks him out as an experienced soldier, even if somewhat of fortune. And it may be that this reputation was
the signal feature which led to his selection as *chef de brigade*.

It is often assumed that he was of Irish extraction, and an American
citizen. But these assumptions about his nationality have been questioned.
The claim that he was a native of Wexford derives from the account written by H.L. Williams in the nineteenth century, and it may be noted again
that much of what he writes, upon which so many other versions have
relied, is of dubious veracity. There is though, in this case, some evidence
to support the notion that he was of Irish birth, or at least extraction. The
Duke of Rutland is an important source of information (mostly gleaned
from Cawdor - the man closest to the matter); and saw a good deal of
Tate, who he describes as 'an old man, and of Irish birth'.[66] In a letter to
the Minister of War dated 19 December 1796 a French General, close to
Hoche, writes that the invasion forces will be commanded by 'Colonel
Irlandois Teate' [sic].[67] But the fact that, with this exception, he is always
referred to in French documentation as 'Colonel Americain', exhaustive
research has led Jones to conclude that 'the balance of evidence seems to
be very much in favour of Tates's being American by birth'.[68] A further
clue lies in the absence of any suggestion that he should be charged with
treason, which would be an obvious course of action if he were Irish. And
neither were those officers in the invasion force who were clearly Irish so
charged (although it was considered). But the absence of any consideration of the labelling of Tate as a traitor is compounded by the absence of
critical documentation, such as any deposition he may have made. Finally,
in his will dated 1792, he leaves property to 'my nephew William Tate son
of my oldest brother Samuel Tate of the Kingdom of Iriland' [sic].[69]

As with his nationality, the question of his age is of some interest. Contemporary accounts centre around seventy, as for example Rutland does, who will have received this information from Cawdor. Stuart Jones notes that in a report of his examination at the Admiralty in *The Courier* of 6 March 1797, he is described as 'above seventy years of age'.[70] An eye-witness wrote to the member of Parliament for Carmarthen that, 'he is an old grey-haired man – has little the appearance of a gentleman'.[71] Another man who saw him was Mr Jenkins who lived near Hay, and who travelled to west Wales to see what was happening there: 'At 7 I saw General Tate conveyed to the Gaol. He was a tall thin old man about 60, was dressed in a long blue Coat faced with Scarlet, blue Pantaloons, white waistcoat, Cocked Hat and National Cockade.'[72]

However, this long held assumption about Tate's age has been put in doubt by a recent discovery by Rose.[73] It was in a 'List of French Officers, Prisoners of War who have been permitted to return to France on Parole since the 13th day of December 1798 … and who are hitherto not exchanged, with Particular Descriptions of their Persons'. Noting that Tate had been released on 24 November 1798, the document describes him as having grey eyes, with a long and pale face, of slim build, 5ft 10in in height, and being forty-four years of age. This entry has some force, since it is in an official document. But this does contradict every other observation made about his age. It is of course possible that this entry was a mistake, which is not uncommon in handwritten historical material, although the only reason to suppose so, is that it is the only suggestion that Tate was some thirty years younger than has always been believed. If the entry *is* correct, then an important puzzle goes some way to being solved. This goes back to the question as to why, with all the young talent available in the revolutionary army, a septuagenarian was chosen to be leader. If in fact he was a good deal younger, then leaving aside the fact that he was not French and could not speak the language of his troops, then his selection does not seem so odd. It also undermines the often expressed belief that the French sent the party they did in order to get rid of them, Tate included: 'However, as Tate was around seventy years of age at this time, and may have been making a bit of a nuisance of himself, one cannot help feeling that Hoche and Carnot may have been glad to get him out of the way.'[74] Hoche though, at least officially, seems to have had faith in him. He wrote to the Directory that:

I have confided to a man of ability, an ex-soldier, the command of the second legion of irregulars, which I have raised as secretly as possible. It is composed of six hundred men from all the prisons in my district, and they are collected in two forts or islands to obviate the possibility of their escape.[75]

The invaders were designated the Deuxième Légion des Francs. As to the troops, Tone saw them and wrote: 'saw the Legion Noire reviewed; about 1800 men. They are the banditti intended for England and sad blackguards they are': 'Spies in Brest reported that they were "fourteen hundred convicts selected from the most abandoned rogues" in the prisons of Rochefort, Nantes, and Lorient, with officers appointed from the most violent Jacobins in Hoche's army.'[77] As to the nature of these troops, in a letter to Cawdor dated 20 March 1797 Le Brun - the aristocrat who in the strange world of the Revolution was second in command of the Legion - claims that there were not as many criminals in the invading force as was generally supposed.[78]

This theme – the criminal, and in many ways contemptible, nature of the invading force – was taken up, and has become a standard feature of the story of the invasion. However, this must be regarded as an exaggeration, to put it mildly. We shall go on to see that almost half were in fact grenadiers, professional soldiers who impressed the Duke of Rutland when he saw them in captivity. Some were children, such as Louis Arnoux who died of 'mortification of the feet' in Pembroke prison. He was thirteen.[79] There were also Irish officers, who it would appear from their later depositions were not criminals, and there were also officers who had been former aristocrats, or in the jargon of the day were of 'gentle birth'. One of these, St Amans, will be discussed in some detail later. And many of these had considerable military experience. One mystery about the composition of the force is that Wolfe Tone records that he recruited 'about fifty Irish and ten English'.[80] The mystery lies in the question as to what became of them. If they actually got as far as Fishguard, why were they not tried for treason? We will see that the authorities were hesitant about putting Irishmen on trial, but there seems no reason not to have done so with the English, or probably more correctly, British.

Since Tate could not speak French, the task of translating the orders drawn up by Hoche was given to Tone. On 25 November 1996 he wrote in his diary that:

> I have been hard at work half this day translating orders and instructions for Col.
> Tate, an American officer ... to go on a buccaneering party into England ...
> the instructions are incomparably well drawn ... and if Tate be a dashing fellow
> with military talents he may play the devil in England before he is caught ...
> the citizens of the Legion Noire are very little behind my countrymen either in
> appearance or morality, which last has been prodigiously cultivated by three or
> four camps in Bretagne and La Vendee. A thousand of these desperadoes ... will
> edify John Bull exceedingly if they get safe into Lancashire.[81]

The next day he wrote that he had made a fair copy of the instructions
which had been altered:

> Particularly with regard to his first destination, which is now fixed to be Bristol.
> If he arrives safe it will be very possible to carry it with a coup de main. I can-
> not but observe here that I transcribed with the greatest sang froid the orders
> to reduce to ashes the third city in the British dominions, in which there is
> perhaps property to the amount of £5,000,000. But such a thing is war.

In the light of subsequent events, which included the seeming inability of
Tate to act when he got ashore in Pembrokeshire and has since been the
ultimate puzzle for historians as to what the purpose of the attack could
have been; and as it seemed devoid of hope from the beginning, it is worth
setting out Hoche's lengthy instructions about the first part of the invasion
in full. It can be seen from these that, whatever the outcome may have
been, Tone was right to have described them as 'incomparably well drawn':

> There will be placed under the command of Col. Tate a body of troops
> completely organized, to the number of one thousand and fifty, all resolute
> determined men, with whom he may undertake anything: they are to be
> called 'La seconde legion de France'. The legion is completely armed. He
> will be likewise furnished with fast going vessels with which he is to proceed,
> before, with, or after the squadron. The vessels will be victualled for the pas-
> sage but the legion will bring on shore nothing but their ammunition which
> is to be musket cartridges. Col. Tate is to have the command in chief of the
> legion; the admiral will give the necessary orders to the officer commanding
> the naval force, which will proceed up St. George's Channel, and the landing
> is to be effectuated, if possible, in or near Cardigan Bay.

But should Col. Tate, on arriving at the mouth of the Severn, learn that the river is little or not at all defended, and that the wind and tide allow him to sail up, he will endeavour to execute a *coup de main* on Bristol, which is the second city in England for riches and commerce; the destruction of Bristol is of the very last importance, and every effort should be made to accomplish it.

For this purpose it will be proper to reconnoitre the mouth of the Severn in the daytime and to sail up the Avon at nightfall within five miles of the town, where the landing should be made on the right bank in the greatest silence and, the troops being supplied with combustible material, Col. Tate is to advance rapidly in the dark on that side of Bristol which may be to windward and immediately to set fire to that quarter. If the enterprise be conducted with dexterity it cannot fail to produce the total ruin of the town, the port, the docks, and the vessels, and to strike terror and amazement into the very heart of the capital of England.

This object being fulfilled, Col. Tate will immediately re-embark, cross the Severn, and land below Cardiff, which he will leave on his right, and proceed towards Chester and Liverpool, in the manner to be pointed out in these instructions. [Salmon's Note; since the expedition never got this far, these are not included here.] During the passage Col. Tate will take care that the troops observe the most exact discipline and will recommend to the naval officers to carry a press of sail.

At the moment of the landing each soldier is to be furnished with one hundred round of ammunition, provisions for four days, and a double ration of wine or brandy, to recruit them after the fatigues of the voyage.

Not a moment is to be lost in the debarkation, and the soldiers must carry their ammunition and provisions until they can secure pack-saddle horses; they are never to quit them and are to take care to supply what may be expended, on every possible occasion. For the first two days the legion is to keep in one body, observing not to suffer any to lag in the rear.

Col. Tate will feel the necessity of gaining a close and strong country with all possible speed and, before committing any act of hostility, he will take care to avoid the morasses, as well as from regard to the health of the troops as to avoid being surrounded by the enemy, who would, of course, endeavour to profit of such a defect in his position.

The expedition under the command of Col. Tate has three objectives. The first is, if possible, to raise an insurrection in the country; the second is to interrupt and embarrass the commerce of the country; and the third is to prepare and facilitate the way for a descent, by distracting the attention of the English government. In all countries the poor are the class most prone to insurrection, and this disposition is to be forwarded by distributing money and drink, by inveighing against the government as the cause of the public distress, by recommending and facilitating a rising to plunder the public stores and magazines and the property of the rich, whose affluence is the natural subject of envy to the poor.

It is, notwithstanding, to be observed that, however defective may be the morality of the English people, they still have a respect for the law and magistrates, even in the moment of insurrection; it will be therefore advisable to spare, as much as possible, the property of those who may be in any civil function, and even of the country gentlemen; all impositions should be laid on the peers, the men of rank and high fortune, the clergy, those who serve as officers in the army, navy, and especially in the militia; of all such the country seats, farms, woods, cattle and corn, should be given up to be plundered by the people. These predatory excursions should be made in different and even distant quarters by detachments of two or three hundred men each.

Extremities such as these, rendered necessary by those of the Republic, and justified by the reflection that our cruel enemy has shewed the first example, will attract numbers of artisans and workmen, of vagabonds and idlers, and even of malefactors, but special care must be taken not to incorporate them into the legion; they are to be formed into new companies commanded by French officers, and to the end that the natives may not be acquainted with the force employed, these companies are to be kept asunder and in ignorance of the details, so far as circumstances will permit, - it is principally by these new formed companies that the insurrection is to be forwarded.

The commerce of the enemy in the country is to be interrupted by breaking down bridges, cutting of dykes, and ruining causeways - (which is, at the same time, essentially necessary for the preservation of the army), by plundering all convoys of subsistence, the public stages and wagons, and even private carriages, the cutting off of the supplies of provisions from the principal towns, burning all vessels and boats in the rivers and canals, destroying magazines, setting fire to docks and coal yards, rope-walks, great manufactories, etc. It is to be observed likewise that, by these means, a crowd of artisans will be thrown out of employment and, of course, ready to embark on any measure which holds out to them subsistence and plunder without labour or fatigue.

The success of the expedition will likewise be forwarded by disarming the militia, by burning the arsenals in the seaports, by stopping the couriers of the government, by seducing the enemy's troops to desert, and by the terror which the success of the legion and the progress of the insurrection will carry into the bosom of the unwarlike citizens. The country most favourable for this system is that which is naturally strong and in which there are forges and manufactures.

Subsistence is to be seized wherever it can be found; if any town or village refuse to supply it in the moment it is to be given up to immediate pillage.

In order to spread the panic as generally as possible the legion is to be divided into several columns having settled a common rendezvous where they are to assemble every four, six, or eight days. The inhabitants must be obliged to serve as guides, and any who refuse are to be punished on the spot. The magistrates or some of their families are to be employed in preference on this service, that they may not accuse or punish the others.

All denunciations against those who join the legion are to be punished by death. Wherever the legion or any of its columns are posted, if the neighbouring parishes do not give instant notice of the approach of the enemy, whether by ringing of bells or otherwise, they are to be given up to fire and sword. For the safety of the troops under his command, Col. Tate will avoid, as much as possible, all engagements with regular forces and will, instead thereof, attack detachments, beat up their quarters, surprise their outposts, etc. He will encourage all deserters and prisoners to enter into the new companies before mentioned. Should such prisoners refuse he will shave their heads and eyebrows, and if they are again taken in arms, they are to be shot.

Col. Tate will not omit to observe that there are in England numbers of French who will be eager to join him, such as prisoners of war, soldiers and sailors, privates in the emigrant regiments, and a crowd of others whom want and the desire of vengeance will draw to his standard. He will admit such Frenchmen into the legion but he will observe to be on his guard that the newcomers may not raise cabals or factions, especially if there should be among them any nobles or priests, whose ambition is to be exceeded only by their cowardice. Should any such attempt be made he will take care to punish it severely. Should the militia or volunteers of any district oppose the march of the legion such district is to be severely punished, the militia or volunteers to be disarmed, their arms to be distributed among the insurgents, and all ammunition carefully preserved.

Finally, Col. Tate will always remember to avail himself of the talents of the principal officers who surround him; he will profit of all favourable circumstances to acquire for his party the force and confidence necessary to ensure success; he will spare, and even maintain, the poor and the aged, the widow and the orphan, and will force the great, who are the cause of all our evils, to sustain the whole burden of the war.[82]

Apart from the fact that this document shows that the expedition, whatever it became, was not initially a 'pantomime' but a serious matter, it is in itself of intrinsic interest. It is written by one of the great figures of the Revolution, and an experienced soldier. We are left with a number of questions, such as why he singles out the officers in the Militia - 'especially in the militia'. And it is interesting, if not surprising, that he warns Tate to watch out for nobles and clergy, and admonishes him that only privates in the emigrant companies should be recruited.

At the time of the invasion, there was still strong support in Britain for the Revolution and its ideals. These were not seriously undermined until the breakdown of the Treaty of Amiens in 1803. This peace treaty, 'the Definitive Treaty of Peace', had only been agreed in 1802. The treaty included agreement about the restoration of French colonies. But serious disagreements soon arose, about the future of the Belgian provinces for example, and war broke out again. There was also the rise to power of Napoleon at the very beginning of the nineteenth century, and for idealists, with the disappointment he brought with his rejection of revolution, and his determined course of imperialism. The ideals of the revolution were forgotten, and the focus became a loathing of the much maligned 'Corsican' in Britain.

But in 1797, the ambitions were considerable: and the orders, set out above, pompous enough. We now go on to see how the orders matched the events.

3

The Invasion

Although the instructions to Tate were clear, the actual purpose of the attack on Pembrokeshire is hardly so. Indeed there is an often expressed view, repeated here, that after the disaster of Bantry Bay, 'Since the original object of creating a diversion from Hoche's expedition no longer applied, it may well be that a desire simply to dispose of such an unsavoury force played a larger role than Anglophobia.'[1]

Yet, although the expedition may appear in retrospect to have been foolhardy, even suicidal, within the terms of reference set out, the objectives were clear. It was to cause as much damage to installations of various kinds as possible, and thus to draw valuable resources away from other areas where they were needed. Indeed this process had begun with military units from other parts of the country being sent to Pembrokeshire when the news broke of the invasion. Had there been a commander of the calibre of Humbert, as we shall go on to see, the disruption and damage could have been considerable.

When the invasion finally took place, it came as a complete surprise to the British government. The belief, and the policy based on that belief, had always been that if an attack were to be made, it would be made in the east of England. It had always seemed obvious that any invasion must be directed at the East Coast, and it was there that defensive installations and troops were concentrated including, a minor paradox - the Pembrokeshire militia being amongst them. The government minister Henry Dundas, Secretary of War, made this policy clear in a *Memorandum on the Coasts and Bays of Great Britain and Ireland and their General Defence*: 'The coast of the Bristol Channel, St. George's Channel & the North of Scotland demand such peculiar and great arrangements to attack them, that they probably do not enter into the contemplation of an Enemy, who has greater objects to aim at nearer at hand.'[2]

The French force was conveyed in four ships: two frigates *La Vengeance* and *La Resistance*, a corvette *La Constance* and a lugger *Le Vatour*. The commander was Commodore Jean Joseph Castagnier, and his log gives details of the voyage.[3] There were several sightings of the fleet as they made their journey. The ships had been seen on their journey off Lundy Island by the master of a sloop, and he reported the sighting to Samuel Hancorne, the collector of the port of Swansea. He duly reported to Portland on 22 February, that the master of the sloop *St Ives* had seen the French ships:

> About two Leagues from the north end of the Island Lundy, which bore from the south west and continued in sight of them until about 4 in the afternoon, at which time they were nearly in the same position but drawn closer together ... further than Mr John commanding the Dolphin Customhouse Cutter stationed at St. Ives, having put to sea on Sunday last saw the same ships and made signal to them, which being unanswered he put back and gave intelligence to the Customhouse there – Mr. Stevens has given these particulars to Capt. Gibbs the Regulating Captain here, who purposes to communicate the same to the Commanding Officer at Plymouth, and, as I conclude to the Admiralty also; being of opinion that they are the Enemies ships reconnoitring, whereof it appeared to me to be advisable to acquaint your Grace.[4]

From Barnstaple came the news in a letter written on 23 February that:

> this Coast and Neighbourhood have been greatly alarmed by the Appearance of three French Frigates & a Luggar ... their Appearance has greatly agitated the minds of all Ranks and brought forth the Volunteer Companies from all the neighbourhood They shew a very loyal and British spirit. Several of the neighbouring Gentlemen have begged leave to attach themselves to my Detachment, should there be any Enemy in these parts.

According to another report, from the commanding officer of the North Devon Regiment of volunteers, the French had 'scuttled several merchantmen, and were attempting to destroy shipping in the harbour', but he does concede that 'this affair may be misrepresented and exaggerated'. Nevertheless he called out his volunteers, and included in his letter the usual fulsome praise of their loyalty, and the satisfaction he feels, 'on seeing the men so willing to defend their king and country, at the same time as silent, orderly and sober as might be expected at a morning parade of an old regiment.'[5]

It is not quite clear what the commanding officer of the North Devons means when he wrote of 'misrepresentation' and exaggeration. The French commander, Castagnier, seems to confirm that he had been active, when he writes that he had to leave Dublin, whither he had gone when he left Cardigan Bay, in part because of bad weather but also because he was 'cumbered with prisoners taken from the fourteen vessels we had sunk'. He also records that because of unfavourable weather he decided to leave the Bristol Channel and make for Cardigan Bay, 'the second place assigned to me for landing the troops'. On Wednesday 22 February 1797 at noon, he saw St David's Head, and at 4 p.m. he anchored in Cardigan Bay. A story associated with the arrival of the fleet off the Pembrokeshire coast alleges that one of the French vessels, flying British colours, went into Fishguard harbour. They were there saluted by the battery in the fort, which the French supposed was an act of aggression. The ship then returned to the shelter of Carreg Wastad.[6]

Rose points out that this story probably emerged in a book entitled *The Fishguard Invasion by the French in 1797: Some passages taken from the Diary of the late Daniel Rowlands, sometime vicar of Llanfiangelpenybont*, published in London in 1892.[7] This, in turn, may have been based upon an incident described by A.L. Williams[8] in which *inter alia*, the firing of a salute is mentioned. This was because the French ships were flying British colours.[9] At 5 p.m. the disembarkation began, in sixteen boats according to Williams, and by 4 a.m. on 23 February the French force had been landed with all their equipment at Carreg Wastad bay.

At 4 p.m. Castagnier reported that Tate 'and his officers informed me that they had no further need of my services' and by 5.10 p.m. the squadron had sailed, leaving the invasion party to their very uncertain fate. The fate of the French ships was no more felicitous, since on 8 March a ship described as a small cutter, but named *Le Vatour* was captured. Salmon thinks that this is not the same lugger that formed part of the invasion fleet, but gives no clear reason for believing that it was not. He notes that the ship which did take part, as well as *La Vengeance*, were captured later in the war. Shortly afterwards, both *La Résistance* and *La Constance* were taken by the *St Florenzo* and the *Nymphe*, in a 'fight that did not last more than half an hour', as recounted in Captain Neale's report to Admiral Lord Bridport. The *Résistance* 'is only six months old, built upon a new construction, and is in every respect one of the finest frigates the French had, and certainly the largest'. *La Constance* 'is two years old and a very fine ship'.[10] No British sailors were killed or wounded and the French lost eighteen men, with fifteen wounded. The disaster attendant upon the capture or destruction of these ships is an important part of the war against Britain. The *Résistance* was brought into service as HMS *Fisguard* – the antique spelling of Fishguard – and was on active service until 1814, including taking part in Nelson's blockade of Toulon.[11]

The weather on 22 February was remarkably warm and clear with a calm sea. Having arrived in the bay, the force scaled the cliff, by no means an easy feat. Fenton describes how, 'Their casks of ammunition, heavy as they were, were rolled up an almost precipitous steep, grown glassy by the dryness of the weather. This was a task apparently so Herculean as almost to exceed credibility.'[12] But they did it, though they lost about eight men. This initial action was reported, via the *Vatour*, which had returned to Brest, and the army commander there, to the Minister of War. The latter was told that Tate had met no opposition and the arrival of the force had terrified the area. He advocated a follow up invasion. The minister was also told of an incident which is not mentioned in any British accounts. It was that Tate, in the presence of the troops, had had a man shot against 'the wall of a house he had pillaged'.[13]

Having reached the top, Lieutenant Barry St Leger, who will become a familiar figure in this narrative, a native born Irishman, was sent on by Tate to establish a headquarters with some of the grenadiers. They did so at Trehowel farm, just under a mile inland. The farmer, John Mortimer, and his staff had already escaped, and the house was locked. A.L. Williams has a more elaborate version. In his, one of the servants Ann George, stated that Mortimer 'was fully persuaded' that the ships which appeared off the coast were English, 'and that the officers would come on shore, and being of a very hospitable disposition, ordered a variety of refreshments to be got ready for their reception and entertainment'.[14] They 'too soon discovered their mistake', and fled. Syd Walters, with his strong belief in treachery, suggests that Mortimer was a traitor, and was prepared for the invaders. And so his version is even more fanciful than that of Williams.[15]

According to St Leger, against his orders the grenadiers smashed their way in, and though he claimed that he had threatened to shoot them, in return they threatened to shoot him. If St Leger is to be believed, and it should be remembered that this claim was made after his capture when there was an even chance that he would be tried for treason, this was an ominous indication of the ill discipline of the troops. Especially since, as grenadiers, it may be assumed that they were the best of the invasion party. Another reason for doubting this officer's evidence is that the invasion instructions drafted by Hoche made clear that the soldiers had to 'forage': 'Subsistence is to be seized wherever it can be found: if any town or village refuse to supply it in the moment it is to be given up to immediate pillage.'[16]

But what was to prove something of a disaster for the French, and a considerable advantage for the local defenders, was that in preparation for his wedding John Mortimer had stocked his house, notably with drink. Incidentally, the availability of drink was increased by the recent wrecking of a Portuguese ship carrying wine, from which many of the locals had stocked up, and which was then drunk by what were to become marauding groups. After a short absence, St Leger returned to Trehowel to find the party already drunk and threatening to burn the hay ricks. He claimed he managed to stop them. When Mortimer returned to his farm he discovered a considerable amount of damage, much of it wanton. For example, the window frames had been burnt, mattresses had been cut up and made into trousers, and a clock had been stolen. A.L. Williams adds an extra extremely unlikely gloss to this story:

> General Tate, seeing the dogs playing about Mr. Mortimer, went out to see him, and asked 'are you the master here?' 'I was so once.' He then said that he had often been in battle, over his shoes in blood; but he had never felt such a sensation as when he put his foot on British ground - that his heart failed him, in a way he could not describe.[17]

Mortimer was luckier than some, since compensation was made. On 27 February, the Home Secretary wrote to Lord Milford:

> I am given to understand that the French troops who landed at Fishguard, previous to their surrender pillaged some of the houses of the Country People in that neighbourhood, and I have in consequence received His Majesty's

Commands to desire that your Lordship will direct a proper enquiry to be made into the particular losses which it may have sustained by the Enemy's Depredations, and that you will report the results to me, for His Majesty's consideration.[18]

But, it was reported that:

It was impossible for us to obtain evidence to contradict those who swore they lost the different articles specified, all we could do, was to lessen where we could, the value of different articles, and tho' there are many *absurd* and *ridiculous* charges, which I am ashamed of, but being stated as *losses*, we conceived it to be our duty to obey His Grace the Duke of Portland's letter.[19] [his italics.]

But under this government scheme, Mortimer claimed £133 10s 6d, a not inconsiderable sum. He was described by Mr Mathias, the adjudicator of claims, as 'a respectable young Farmer, bearing the Character of a very honest man'.[20] His claim was honoured.

When the invasion happened Colonel Thomas Knox, commanding officer of the Fishguard Volunteers, was at a ball at a prosperous farmhouse Tregwynt, some four miles from where the landing took place. Tregwynt was then occupied by a well known, indeed distinguished Pembrokeshire family, called Harries. And here is a first hand version of what happened:

Miss Mary Gwynne Harries, whom the writer [Nelson George Harries] met at Tenby on 29th March, 1902, and who was then about 80 years old, remembered having been at Tregwynt before 1830. She knew a Mrs. Bird who was a niece of an old servant of the family who was lady's maid to Mrs. George Harries and in the house on the night of the ball in 1797. This servant told Mrs. Bird that she was serving tea in an ante-room on the news of the French landing and that the hostess and guests at once took to their carriages and horses, leaving the lights all burning and the supper just laid on the table. The only one who remained was an old member of the family said to have been in the Army, who said that he would wait for the French, and did so, having loaded all the firearms in the place ... Mrs. Harries with her two sons, George and Thomas Frederick, got into their coach with what valuables they could collect and drove to Narbeth.[21]

This lively account communicates well the surprise, and fear, the announcement of the invasion must have incurred.

Knox went to Trehowel, to try to discover what was happening. He saw the French ships, and upon going to Fishguard he met people fleeing the area, all convinced that the French had landed. Knox still seems not to have been convinced, but he nevertheless sent a message to Major Bowen to bring the Newport Division of the Volunteers to the village of Dinas, between Fishguard and Newport. Knox has been criticised for this apparent hesitation,[22] but it was the first of a number of decisions on his part which, as we go on to see, was to lead to bitter arguments, much vituperation, and even challenges to duels. It was the arrival of a man who had been captured and wounded by the French which eventually convinced Knox that there was indeed an invasion party on the cliffs. By this time a message had been sent to the Lord Lieutenant, Lord Milford at Picton, This was followed by a message from Knox, telling Milford that he intended to attack in the morning, if he judged that the numbers justified the risk.

The news had by now reached Haverfordwest and a committee met in the Castle Inn (now the Castle Hotel) to decide what to do. The commanding officer of the Pembrokeshire Militia was Lieutenant Colonel Colby, and it was largely due to his initiative that actions were set in motion. Fortunately, although the Militia were on duty in Harwich, Colby was in Pembrokeshire to train some of the Militia. The Cardiganshire Militia were ordered from Pembroke where they had been guarding prisoners of war, Ackland was ordered to bring the Pembroke Volunteers, and Cawdor the Pembrokeshire (Castlemartin) Yeomanry. We have come across the name of Captain Longcroft in connection with the rioting Hook miners of 1795, for it was on that occasion when his men 'pressed' a recalcitrant miner, who shortly, and no doubt to his surprise, found himself at sea. On this occasion he managed to draw on some small ships, as well as his own press gang, to contribute to the forces ranged against the French. He also reinforced Haverfordwest with cannons from naval vessels.[23] One under sung contribution to this 'sea force' was that made by the customs service. At this time, this service was quite distinct from the Royal Navy, and although Cawdor refers to them as lieutenants and captains 'these appear to have been courtesy titles'.[24] There were two revenue cutters at Milford, one of which, it is said, encountered the French fleet while on patrol. The commander returned to Milford and reported his sighting. The commander of the *Speedwell*, Commander Hopkins, 'lost no time in unshipping some of his cutter's guns in readiness for their cross-country journey to Fishguard'.[25] The efforts of the two commanders were commended in a letter from Cawdor to the Board of Customs on 14 March:

> Sir,
>
> I think it my duty to have the honour of addressing you upon an occasion highly gratifying to me, and which I am confident will give great satisfaction to your Honourable Board, to express the high sense I entertain of the alacrity and determined spirit of all your officers and men in the two ports of Milford Haven, upon the late occasion of the French effecting a landing in Pembrokeshire … particularly recommending … Lieut. Hopkins of the *Speedwell* cutter, to whose extraordinary exertions in landing guns etc. from the vessel he commanded, the surprising expedition with which he brought them forward a distance of more than 27 miles and in short for the whole of his spirited and officer-like conduct: the conduct of Lieut. Dobbin of the *Diligence* cutter, to whom I think the Service highly indebted for exertions that do credit to the profession to which he has the honour to belong, and which will ever call for my grateful remembrance.[26]

The secretary to the Board of Customs wrote to express his pleasure at the thanks that had been received. He also assured the admiralty that the commissioners 'would be giving urgent consideration to the manner in which the officers should be rewarded for their zeal'.[27]

At this juncture it will be useful to set out the composition of the forces comprising the defence of Pembrokeshire. The first point to be noted is that, apart from the small contingent of seamen, none of the defenders were professional or experienced soldiers. The exigencies of the war, and its attendant phenomenon, the expansion of empire, meant that the regular army units were on duty overseas. There were three regular regiments which were later to have local, Welsh, connections. These were the 23rd (The Royal Welch Fusiliers), the 24th who in 1881 became the South Wales Borderers, and the 41st, to be designated The Welch Regiment in 1831. In 1797 the 23rd were in the east of England, *inter alia*, helping to suppress the naval mutiny at the Nore, the 24th were in Canada, and the 41st had just returned from the West Indies. It is to be supposed that the presence of the regular army would have been desirable, although it is a commonplace that their morale was low, and their behaviour unpredictable. It was a constant battle to keep order, and every kind of tactic was used to that end. On the King's birthday in 1797, when the 23rd were sent to prevent naval mutineers landing, an address was sent to the King stating:

> How much we detest the infamous attempts made on the minds of the army of late, in the distribution of certain seditious handbills. We are happy to say that no atrocious villain has ever yet been daring enough to attempt by arti-fice (or otherwise) to seduce the Royal Welch Fuzileers from their hitherto unerring fidelity.[28]

The defence of Pembrokeshire relied therefore on locally raised units, some of whom were volunteers and some of whom were conscripted.

The conscripted men consisted of militia, in this case the Cardiganshire Militia. Under a series of Acts, beginning in 1757 civilians had to serve for a period in the Militia, an arrangement which had all the ingredients to cause enormous discontent. The system was selective, by ballot, and those selected could pay for a substitute to be enrolled. In Pembrokeshire there was difficulty in recruiting, even though Lord Milford person-ally gave extra money to encourage it.[29] The protest against service took the form of serious rioting in many parts of the country, includ-ing Carmarthenshire at the end of 1796.[30] Nevertheless, west Wales had to raise its units. Pembrokeshire and Carmarthenshire did so in 1759, and Cardiganshire in 1760. It was the latter regiment that were to range against the French invaders.

The problem with the Militia was the same as that with the regu-lar army. They were often unreliable, mutinous, and prone to side with the mob they were supposed to quell. It was for this reason that the local 'home' unit was rarely used when there was a disturbance in their own district. We saw that in the case of the riot by Hook miners, it was the Carmarthenshire Militia who were called in, and would have been quite happy to use their weapons against the rioters, since as south Pembrokeshire people they would have been regarded as foreigners, or as in one well-used phrase, 'Pembrokeshire pigs'.

And so the Militia system was so resented that it led to riots. In March 1770, in Chirk, there was such a riot when an attempt was made to enforce enlistment. On that occasion:

A noisy 400 - 500 strong mob gathered outside, armed with knotted ash clubs, pitchforks and rakes, broke the windows of the room occupied by the magistrates and declared they would take away their lives if they persisted in the execution of the warrant to ballot for militia men. When the justices went outside to reason with the people their efforts proved in vain.

The magistrates were forced to agree that people should be exempted from service for the remainder of the three years. Later their demands went further with a statement that they should be exempt for good. When a magistrate said that legally he could not allow this, he was warned that: 'Next time the authorities should meet for the purpose they would come down with ten times the number and kill all of them.'[31]

In the light of such hatred it is not surprising that the history of the Militia is full of examples of indiscipline. In 1800 a note was distributed amongst the west London Militia saying 'we had better dy by the sword than starve in the land of plenty'[32]. The situation is well summed up by Western who wrote, 'Law breaking was rampant ... men deserted in shoals' and there was a 'chronic state of insubordination'.[33]

Another branch of the armed services called into being because of the war were the Volunteers. Nationally, they were intended to act as a military reserve. But like the other units raised in the second half of the century, as well as the practice in the regular army, they would be used to curb civil revolt. 'For the Government's military planners, the Volunteers were mainly an instrument of repression'.[34] An example precisely from Pembrokeshire, is the keeping of peace in Haverfordwest in the days following the riot of Hook miners in 1795. Then the Fishguard Volunteers were called in when the Carmarthen Militia left. In fact their existence was politically controversial for conflicting reasons. On the one hand:

The Volunteers were in fact the perfect cadres for political clubs. The brilliant uniforms they affected were a splendid piece of propaganda in themselves, impressive to the onlooker and tickling the vanity of the recruit. The parades and days of exercises were a perfect setting and pretext for patriotic speeches.[35]

One association observed that the Volunteers 'encouraged and restored a due principal of subordination amongst the different classes of the people' and 'rendered disloyalty unfashionable, sedition dangerous and insurrection almost impossible'.[36] On the other hand, there was a worry that such service might make 'people more politically conscious' with the attendant danger of revolt.[37] Apart from the fun of display, being a Volunteer brought a major advantage - that it meant exemption from the loathsome Militia call-up.[38] It is interesting in this connection, that the largest of the units parading against the French at Fishguard were the local Volunteers.

The Fishguard Volunteers are often called the Fishguard Fencibles, the latter being a term which Bryn Owen points out as incorrect in this case, although both terms are used in literature in respect of the Fishguard unit.[39] The term 'Fencible' means strictly troops who were enlisted for service within the country, and not for service overseas, and who served for the duration of the war. The Fishguard unit, it will be remembered, was raised by Knox senior. There were also three officers and ninety-three members of another volunteer group, the Pembroke Volunteers. The commanding officer of this detachment was Captain James Ackland, who has already been mentioned.

Finally there were the Yeomanry. Because of the strains resulting from the war, Pitt made a speech in March 1794 in which he announced an increase in the forces. Part of this strategy was the proposal to put together cavalry units comprising 'Gentlemen, Yeomen, Farmers and substantial Tradesmen'. Naturally he did not say so, but this had little to do with the defence of the realm against external enemies, but a good deal to do with the control of an increasingly desperate civil population. He came near to the truth in Section VI of the plan which stated that this unit was to be called out 'for the suppression of riots or tumults within their own or adjacent counties'.[40] The Pembrokeshire Yeomanry were often called upon to do so from patrolling markets to action against the Rebecca Rioters of west Wales in the mid-nineteenth century.

The response to Pitt's idea was immediate on the part of the Pembrokeshire landowners. Lord Milford convened a meeting in London at which it was resolved to form the 'Pembrokeshire Company of Gentlemen and Yeomanry Cavalry'. The speed with which this was done caused the accolade of being the first regiment of yeomanry being accorded to the Pembrokeshire (Castlemartin) yeomanry Hussars, when a precedence list of the Yeomanry regiments was drawn up in 1919.[41] For the purposes of this narrative, the unit will be referred to as the Pembrokeshire Yeomanry.

In the 1930s, supposing that the Yeomanry would welcome the chance to fight, one loyal author made clear his low opinion of the social discontent which was rife in the area, and wrote that, 'A greater destiny awaited this handful of volunteers than the browbeating of disgruntled yokels in their own counties.'[42] And indeed it was the browbeating of 'yokels' that was the main task of the local Yeomanry. Faced with a real army they seem to have been remarkably inactive.

There would have been reinforcements, had any fighting taken place. At first, in neighbouring Carmarthenshire, the news was greeted with disbelief. Cawdor's close friend John Vaughan, who was Lord Lieutenant of the county, wrote for confirmation: 'I have long thought them mad, but till now never considered them to be such fools as to choose such a miserable spot. I am inclined to think this imaginary fleet will prove to be a miserable Privateer intent on plundering a few sheep and starved cattle.'[43]

Nevertheless, he ordered the call out of the Militia, and the Yeomanry, and any others available, so that '5000 would have appeared in a short time'.[44] In addition, units from further away were on the march, such as the New Romney Fencible Cavalry.

The French had seemingly little, if any, idea of the opposition that they would face, and their hope rested upon experience from the Revolution that there was sufficient anger amongst the people to cause them to join their ranks. It has been shown earlier in this narrative that this was their expectation, and even local people turned to this expectation as an explanation for certain events. Thus, John Mends, writing from Haverfordwest at the time, describes hidden arms and ammunition with some bewilderment, but suggests an explanation:

> Since I wrote the above there is arrived in H. West from Fishguard 16 Carts Loaded with kegs of Gunpowder which the French hid in the Caves of the rocks there, and our people says that there is as much hid there which will be brought in tomorrow, and about 2 thousand Stand of arms hid in the Sands in Chests, which will be brought in allso tomorrow Those arms & amonition [sic] was intended to arm all the Country people that would join the French, who says they was promised before they Left Brest to be joined by Some thousands of Welch people, but how that was promised no body knows, or by whom, but this [is] fact as to the Concealment of the arms and ammunition, but to what purpose is unknown at present.[45]

The number of troops defending (and the term is not too overblown) were small. The numbers mobilised to face the invaders in total were: non-commissioned officers and men: Cawdor's Yeomanry 43, Cardigan Militia 100, Pembroke Volunteers (Fencibles) 93, Knox's Fishguard Volunteers (Fencibles) 191 and the naval contingent 150. There were a total of sixteen officers. The total force therefore was 593, although some accounts vary slightly. Owen, for example, wrote that there were seven officers from the naval and revenue services.[46] 593 is likely to be the most accurate count, since this is an official return.[47] This then was the defending force, but as they were dispersed all over the countryside, as part-timers, their attendance was uncertain, and of course communication was difficult.

The number of men in the invasion force was not known. It could have been a massive force. There was no way of knowing. Knox estimated 800 – 900, but this was to prove an underestimate.[48] Rose quotes a French source, which is a document signed by Tate and the senior officers, and countersigned by Hoche himself. Dated 11 December 1796 the total here is 1,229.[49] Given the nature of the organisation, the variable quality, and the erratic behaviour of the French troops, this may well have changed before the invasion was mounted. Some further information about the invading force is found in a document which sets out its structure. It also gives the full names of the officers and their ranks and posts in the force and the total number which was forty-eight. But reports of numbers vary. Dale-Jones, points out that one discrepancy, that of Cawdor's at thirty-six, is probably due to the latter not counting the *Sous Lieutenants* as officers.[50] In the event, the generally accepted number of the entire force is that given by Lieutenant General Rooke to the Duke of Portland, which is 1,224.[51]

Colby rode to Fishguard, spoke to Knox, and advised him to send out scouting parties in civilian clothes to try to discover the strength of the enemy. He also advised him to parade his men on some heights where they could be seen by the French, a tactic which might make them hesitant to advance. Colby then went back to Haverfordwest where the troops were eating and drinking on the Castle Square before marching north. By the time that march had begun, Knox had begun his retreat from Fishguard, a decision he made and for which he was to pay dearly in the aftermath. He based this decision on intelligence, including from a captured Frenchman, that the number of the enemy was between 1,200 and 1,400. His judgement was that his small force could not engage such a large number, and so he decided to retreat towards Haverfordwest and join up with the main column. As part of his later defence he stated that the invasion 'committee' had sent him a message, which was subsequently verified by the messenger who carried it, 'that they thought it most advisable for you to retreat towards Haverfordwest'.[52]

Meanwhile, Lord Cawdor had heard the news in the late evening the night before (the 22nd), and for his part immediately started mobilising the troops in his district, and after crossing Pembroke by ferry spoke to Lord Milford, suggesting that he (Cawdor) should take overall command. To this Milford agreed, since he was in very poor health, although he was only about fifty-five. He suffered especially from gout, as Lady Milford had at one point reported to the Duke of Portland. But this became a contentious issue, since Milford changed his mind on the basis that Colby was the most senior Lieutenant Colonel in the county, and so, obviously in some bemused state, appointed Colby. The latter then told Knox about his appointment who was very surprised because he thought *he* was in command. After much discussion, which must have been acrimonious, and which could not have helped in the circumstances, Colby agreed to submit to Cawdor, and Knox agreed to do the same. So at last the column was on its way to Fishguard.

In the French camp there was some movement. Tate ordered the disposition of troops on some of the commanding heights, such as Carnwnda, which offers a marvellous view of the countryside for miles around. They also prepared an ambush below Carn Gelli, within a short distance from the Haverfordwest to Fishguard road and, 'This point, some two miles from the landing place, represented the limit of the advance on British soil.'[53] Many of the troops were sent out ostensibly to forage, to get horses and so on. This degenerated into plundering and doing physical damage:

> Not a fowl was left alive, and the geese were literally cooked in butter. They then proceeded to plunder, and give loose to every brutal excess that pampered and inflamed appetites could prompt them to; but the veil of night was drawn over their execrable orgies, disgraceful to nature, and which humanity shudders to imagine.[54]

The French tried to enter Manorowen, the home of Rev. David Jones, rector of Llangan in Glamorgan.

Not succeeding there, they went to a farmhouse near by called Trellewelyn. The family fled and locked the door, but a servant hid in a tree and watched the attempt to batter in the door with a large stone. One soldier 'turning his back [to the door], pounded at it between his legs with all his might'. The servant fired at him and missed, but fear of an ambush drove the French away. They were later captured by the local militia. Quite who these 'local militia' were is not clear. The Reverend Jones returning home from Fishguard at the time, saw about twenty of them sitting on the ground, surrounded by their captors, and said, 'Let me have a look at the little black devils'. They were then taken to prison.[55]

In St David's, it has been claimed, there was a spontaneous demand for action. This took the form of a demand from the inhabitants that the lead should be stripped from the roof of the cathedral to make bullets. Not surprisingly this was initially refused, 'but a loyal Welshman came forward, cried out "Church, King, and Constitution", and said that unless the keys were handed over, the people would forcibly strip the cathedral of its lead. This patriotic appeal seems to have prevailed.' The lead was supposedly made into bullets, and this particular myth is reinforced by a story that when a farmhouse called Martell Mill was undergoing alterations, a bag of bullets were found in a wall with a note which read that they had been cast in 1797 for use against the French.[56] Unfortunately the source for this story is again H.L. Williams, and as always, though appealing, is hearsay.

A more credible story, even though it is also to be found in Williams, is that a Liverpool engineer called Henry Whitesides was engaged in building the Smalls lighthouse off the Pembrokeshire coast. This was, incidentally, a difficult and dangerous undertaking, during which he and some of his workers were stranded and would have died, had one of a series of messages they put into the sea in casks not landed and been discovered. Fenton recounts how Whitesides put a distress message into a bottle and the bottle into a cask. Three casks were put into the sea, one coming ashore in Galway, one at Newgale in Pembrokeshire, and, 'the third, most providentially was, in a few days after it left the Smalls, taken up in a creek under Mr. Williams' house, so that immediate assistance was given to the distressed.'[57] He was called by Fenton 'a most ingenious mechanic'.[58] Whitesides called together a group of seamen at Solva, and led them to the scene of the action. H.L. Williams adds that they 'were joined on the march by several hundreds',[59] although there is no further mention of them in the subsequent encounter. They met a party of five French soldiers, and Whitesides is supposed to have said (variously) that they should take their time and aim well (H.L. Williams), or more precisely '"Take care my boys and do it well, faith I am afraid they will kill Mr. Barzey's horse!" The horse which he rode'.[60] One of the Frenchmen was killed, two wounded, and the rest ran off. The Frenchman was buried in a field which was then called Parc-y-Ffrancwr (French field), which field is marked and named on the latest Ordnance Survey map. At this point the:

> French took to their heels. 'Now, boys, load again' cried their gallant leader,
> 'and pursue the rascals'. They were on the point of coming up with the three
> French who remained, when suddenly a party of 15 or 18 others came in
> sight. 'Now is your time to fire and then run for it'. The second fire had no
> effect, but they escaped safely from the enemy and brought away the accou-
> trements of the man they had killed as a trophy. The leader of the Welshmen,
> disdaining to have any advantage over his comrades in their flight, alighted
> and turned his horse adrift.[61]

Although the essence of this story is probably true, like many of the others, the detail is probably fictional. It is, for example, in the nature of things unlikely that anyone would cast away a resource as valuable as a horse. It is claimed that this encounter was witnessed by Tate himself, and this caused him to say that:

> He had often seen soldiers advance, but he had never before witnessed the
> advance of raw, undisciplined men, and that if they could show so bold and
> steady a front and fight so well, what had he to expect from British soldiers
> – that his fourteen hundred men would make but a poor stand against such
> courageous fellows.[62]

Once again, unfortunately, the source of this story is H.L. Williams. This is obviously the same incident described by Rutland with some variation:

> Five countrymen on their way to join the English army (their leader being
> on horseback) met suddenly a party of five Frenchmen, who had been

marauding in a field. They had amongst them four guns, the French were all well armed. Their leader who was nothing more than a common peasant, desired them to all stand firm. Knowing that one of the others could take better aim than himself he gave him his gun, and desired them all to be cool. 'Now, my boys', cried he, 'is your time; be collected, and take good aim'. They did so and fired. One of the French party was killed on the spot, another desperately wounded, and a third slightly hurt. The French on this took to their heels.[63]

There was another skirmish near Carnwnda, where two locals met a group of Frenchmen. Both the locals and one of the Frenchmen were killed.[64] Another example Rutland gives as 'one of the instances of particular courage', describes an episode when a Frenchman had been plundering a cottage, and 'having taken everything he could', asked for bread and cheese. As he was eating it:

The peasant creeped up by degrees to a corner of the cottage, whence he took a thick club, and then sidling up to his enemy, gave him such a blow on the head as laid him totally motionless. He then made his escape after disarming the man. This Frenchman being asked, when afterwards on his march with the rest of his countrymen to the prisons that were prepared for them, by what accident he was covered with blood; he replied – 'Ah! Monsieur, c'est seulement un coup de bâton; cela se passera bientôt!' He was then pale as death, and fainting from the loss of blood.[65]

An especially noteworthy case of vandalism was what the invaders did to St Gwyndaf's church in the tiny village of Llanwnda. The church is very near to the landing place, and was badly damaged, and the invaders destroyed the church documentation and records, possibly to light fires. This seems very likely, and understandable, especially since they had to light fires to keep warm, and possibly to cook. The silver communion set was stolen, and appears to have turned up in Carmarthen. It is commonly claimed that a French officer tried to sell the cup and plate, and 'was at once consigned to gaol, and the cup and plate returned to the Churchwardens'.[66] A guide to the church which was in circulation in 2006 states that, 'The church silver was stolen, but was recovered from a pawn shop in Carmarthen, pawned by person or persons unknown!'

Amongst the more detailed fantasy promulgated by H.L. Williams is that:

Mr. George Probert being appointed Commissary at Carmarthen, he met a French officer in the street, when he offered him a Communion Silver Cup and Plate; he said he had brought them from Lanundee in France. Mr. P told him it was sacrilege - had robbed the church at Llawnda near the camp. Mr Probert returned the cup and the plate to the churchwardens at Llanwnda.[67]

As well as all the theft, violence and killing, there were two rapes, and the treatment by writers of these episodes is rather odd, not to say offensive. At Cotts Farm there was a woman lying in bed with a new born infant. It has been suggested by Laws that her 'cowardly husband' had run away[68], and claims that this report is from contemporaries. But this is described as 'unkind' by Stuart Jones.[69] But then Jones is always reluctant to ascribe bad behaviour of any sort to local people. The woman asked for mercy and showed them the newborn and the soldiers did not harm her, although one version is that they 'removed the available stock of wine'.[70]

Mary Williams of Caerlem was not so lucky. When she saw soldiers moving towards the house, she tried to escape, and was shot in the leg. Stuart Jones, rather coyly, writes that 'she was otherwise ill-treated'.[71] Rutland is more direct, reporting that she was two months pregnant, they shot her in the leg, and she was 'ravished ... in the presence of her husband'.[72] Later she was awarded 'a fat government pension ... which made it well worthwhile',[73] and Jones expresses the same bizarre sentiments when he writes 'financially she did very well out of the invasion, and survived the event to enjoy her pension for fifty six years'.[74] Carradice says that Mrs Williams 'was granted a pension by the Government ... of forty pounds per annum: she continued to claim it for the next fifty six years!' (his exclamation).[75] No doubt this figure was drawn from H.L. Williams who was as sneering as other commentators when he wrote that 'she has consequently received eighteen hundred pounds sterling!'.[76] The official investigator into losses, Mr Mathias reports that he took two affidavits of two women 'who suffered by acts of violence', and notes that Mrs Williams was shot after her rape.[77]

Rutland also described another rape, which is rarely mentioned, although as has just been stated, claims included affidavits from *two* women 'who suffered by acts of violence'.[78] It was, Rutland writes, of 'a virgin sixty years old'. The rapist is named by Rutland as St Leger, one of the Irish officers, the same man who led the assault on Trehowel, and who reappears as a witness in the aftermath. 'This man afterwards informed Lord Cawdor, that he only came over for that amusement, and intended no harm to anyone'.[79] Not only does Rutland definitely quote Cawdor, but the latter may well have heard the details from St Leger himself, since when St Leger was in ColdBath Fields prison in Middlesex, Cawdor visited him, as he did Tate, Tyrell and Le Brun on several occasions as his diary shows.[80]

As time went on, the chaos, which was the seminal reason for the surrender, in the French camp increased. It was related to Rutland that a local whose house had been plundered (according to Stuart Jones he had been personally robbed),[81] and whom he named as a Mr Thomas, a farmer from nearby Mathry, had ventured out to see how his relatives had fared. He was robbed of his silver watch, his shoe buckles, and his money. Another version is that he was:

> an English gentleman, residing in the vicinity of Fishguard [who] went among the French banditti and assured them, in the French language, that there was not the least chance of success as they had a very resolute and hardy people to contend with. They answered him that they came, not as enemies, but to relieve their oppressed brethren.[82]

They then robbed him. He then went into the French camp and complained to an officer, or some claim, to Tate in person. Tate ordered the culprit to be shot, but the soldiers refused to do so arguing that they:

> were only obeying the orders received from their government, which were, to burn and destroy everything they could. Three officers immediately offered to shoot the man. The soldiers on this threatened that if they did, to fire upon their officers. This intimidated the latter, and the point was given up. The man however was detected stealing from his comrades the next day, and the same soldiers, who had the day before refused to execute him, now cut his throat, and threw him over the cliffs. They behaved with great cruelty towards their own people.[83]

Rutland relates another episode in which an officer ordered a grenadier who had broken his thigh to move. He was not able to and 'he was immediately cut down, and his body thrown into the sea'.[84]

By nightfall on the evening of Thursday 23 February, the local troops had arrived and were settled in Fishguard. Later that evening, Tate had decided to surrender, and sent his second in command, Baron de Rochemure, and his ADC Francois L'Hanhard (misspelled by H.L. Williams as Leonard),[85] who could speak English, to find Knox whom he assumed to be in command, and to offer to surrender with the condition that the entire force should be returned to France. They were guided by Thomas Williams of Caerlem, whose wife had been shot and raped, to a house which in later years was to become, and remains, a public house in Fishguard, called the Royal Oak. They met Knox, explained their mission, and handed over a letter which read:

> Cardigan Bay,
> 5th of Ventôse, 5th year of the Republic
>
> Sir,
> The circumstances under which the Body of the French troops under my Command were landed at this place renders it unnecessary to attempt any military operations, as they would tend only to Bloodshed and Pillage. The Officers of the whole Corps have therefore intimated their desire of entering into a Negociation upon Principles of Humanity for a surrender. If you are influenced by similar Considerations you may signify the same by the Bearer, and, in the mean Time, Hostilities shall cease.
> Health and Respect,
> Tate,
> Chef de Brigade.
> To the Officer commanding His Britannick Majesty's Troops

There then took place a discussion between the senior officers, and perhaps because of that discussion, or possibly on Cawdor's own initiative, it was decided to reject the approach which would in any case have appeared ludicrous in London, and to insist on unconditional surrender. Whatever took place in the discussion, as the officer commanding, Cawdor had to take the decision. Although Rose points out that there is evidence that Cawdor had been up to Pencaer, watched the plundering of a house, and captured a French soldier, 'who was so drunk & alarmed that nothing could be got from him',[86] Cawdor must have been still unsure of the strength of the French, or of their quality. And although he could expect reinforcements, the distances were great and there was no way of knowing when they might arrive. Nor would he have known what their quality would be or how they would behave. The certainty was that they would not be regular troops. And, as we shall go on to see, he could not be sure how the local population would respond if there was a fight, and the French appeared to be winning. Little was known, if anything, of the chaos in the French camp, the gross intoxication of the invaders or, as it emerged, the excellent quality of their weapons. So he gambled, and his courage in doing so is a considerable credit to him. Nothing can diminish that. At some point,[87] Ackland delivered a reply to Tate which read:

> Fishguard,
> February 23rd 1797
> Sir,
> The Superiority of the Force under my Command, which is hourly increasing, must prevent my treating upon any Terms short of your surrendering your whole Force Prisoners of War. I enter fully into your Wish of preventing an unnecessary Effusion of Blood, which your speedy Surrender can alone prevent, and which will entitle you to that Consideration it is ever the Wish of British Troops to show an Enemy whose numbers are inferior.
>
> My Major will deliver you this letter and I shall expect your Determination by Ten o'clock, by your Officer, whom I have furnished with an Escort, that will conduct him to me without Molestation.
> I am &c.,
> Cawdor.
> To the Officer Commanding the French Troops.[88]

H.L. Williams mistakenly attributes this demand for unconditional surrender to Knox.[89]

As the local troops were being deployed, Tate agreed to surrender. The surrender was to take place on Goodwick Sands, and the local troops were deployed so as to make the most impressive appearance. Having received Tate's message, Cawdor rode over to Trehowel to receive the surrender from Tate. Rutland reported that, 'Tate was very much confused and frightened when he gave up his sword to Lord Cawdor, who delivered it to his groom, and assured him he should find every protection in his power.'[90]

Stuart Jones discovered a further document about the surrender, signed by the French officers and Tate, which was clearly designed to offset any reprisals that they might meet when they returned to France. It was found in Tate's dossier in French archives. It is published in French as Appendix III of Stuart Jones' book, and it is sufficiently important to be reproduced here in English:

> Today, the 7th Ventose [March] in the Fifth Year of the French Republic, we, the Officers comprising the two Battalions of the Second French Legion, given the insubordination of the troops, the total lack of subsistence, the impossibility of obtaining any; finally the impossibility of raising the resistance necessary for success against the enemy, who has risen en masse with troops of the line amounting to several thousand, whereas we have only twelve hundred, which diminishes every day due to illness and desertion; given, finally, the outrages by which several soldiers, who could not be identified fired rifle shots at their superiors; We, the assembled officers, convinced of the praiseworthy conduct, integrity and justice of Citizen Tate, *Chef de Brigade* commanding the Second French Legion, confirm that he used all means necessary and likely to restore good order, and that, in spite of all his efforts and ours together, being unable to attain the goal to which honour and glory summon us, he has been obliged, following the ultimatum of the English General, to surrender as a prisoner of war. In testimony of which we have written and signed the present document to serve him as he may need it.
>
> Signed by the Officers.
>
> Tate, *Chef de Brigade* of the 2nd French Legion.

On Goodwick sands the scene was pathetic. Having stacked their arms, the prisoners waited until there were boats to carry them round to Fishguard:

> Many of them were at this time very ill of a flux, which they had brought over with them, and some of them died. Their manner of burying the dead was savage in the extreme. After digging trenches, they threw the bodies in without ceremony. One of the bodies happened to be too long, and would not readily fit the grave dug for it … and jumping upon the neck of the dead man, they broke it, and then doubled it back upon the body.[91]

Lieutenant General Rooke, who was sent to Pembrokeshire to take over, wrote to Portland on 3 March that the total number of prisoners was 1,224: 'This is the most trustworthy statement of the number of prisoners or [what is practically the same thing] of the number of Tate's men. All the other statements are more or less approximate guesses but this is obviously an official return made after proper enquiry.'[92]

Eventually, the officers having been separated from the men for reasons of mutual safety as well as security, the fifteen mile march to Haverfordwest began. The French officers went by a different route, the most senior on horseback. The officers, including Tate were confined in the Castle Inn where 'they stayed up all night'.[93] The next day, 25 February, the majority (forty-three) were sent on to Carmarthen, where upon arrival on 26 February they stayed at the historic Ivy Bush Inn, which was the best hotel in the town. As Dale-Jones points out, although such luxury may to the modern eye used to brutal treatment of prisoners seem extraordinary, this was consonant with the code of the time.[94] Portland, again reflecting the values of the day, warned against the seeming nature of rank:

> As certain intelligence has been received that all French troops who were landed in Pembrokeshire were composed of convicts of various descriptions and that those to whom the rank of officer had been given were persons of the same description ... you may be put upon your guard against showing those who are in the garb of officers any of those civilities to which their rank would otherwise induce you.[95]

The officers stayed in the Ivy Bush until 28 February, and were then put in prison. The reason for this was a (false) rumour of another French landing in St David's and the Gower which, in the light of the huge surprise experienced in Pembrokeshire, could not be ignored. General Rooke wrote to Vaughan, the Lord Lieutenant of Carmarthenshire: 'You will be pleased to take charge of the prisoners now at Carmarthen and use the best means to keep them in security as a report is previously here that the enemy is landing.'[96] The result was that on 1 March the Ivy Bush was surrounded by the local Carmarthenshire troops, and in the midst of considerable confusion and anxiety, the officers were transferred to the gaol.

Their behaviour in Carmarthen had been so bad that the Mayor had written to Portland on 27 February that he believed the French prisoners at Haverfordwest were to be sent to England:

I hope that this may be the case, if they are left in this poor country, inevitable
ruin must follow. The loyalty of the people here is beyond description. We
have too many French officers here. Your Grace would render us essential
service if they were sent farther into the country.

He suggests, as those who do not want delinquents in the neighbourhood always do, that they should be sent elsewhere, 'Hereford and Brecon
are two very proper places'.[97] Carmarthen, in any case, had held French
prisoners since the war with France had begun, and their upkeep had to
be sustained by the town.

On 2 March Cawdor and his party began their journey to London 'in
three chaises':

In the first Joe [captain] Adams had charge of Tate and Captain Tyrell, – the
first alarmed and confused, the second a stupid Paddy; I had Le Brun with me,
as dirty as a pig, but more intelligent and better manners; in the last Lord E
Somerset had the care of Captain Norris [actually Morrison] and Lieutenant
St. Leger, both greatly frightened; they had but little conversation.[98]

Le Brun was in fact a French aristocrat, whose real name was Le
Baron de Rochemure. He was a professional soldier in both the pre-
revolutionary, and the revolutionary armies, and had a colourful career,
including service in the British-led army which was beaten at Quiberon,
the event which gave Hoche his long lasting hatred of Britain. Despite
being an aristocrat, in tune with the bizarre atmosphere of the time, Le
Brun was second in command to Tate.[99] Tyrell and Norris 'both confess
themselves Irish and have been many years in France'. St Leger was 'Irish,
but calls himself American – was of Tate's selection for this expedition – a
Young Man'.[100] The Irishmen had every reason to be frightened, since they
were manifestly British subjects, and as far as they knew, could be charged
with treason. Three of the officers were 'examined', in Whitehall and
made statements about themselves. St Leger said that he was 'near twenty
years old', that he was born in Limerick, and that when he was about
twelve he went to live with his uncle in Charlestown in south Carolina.
After a series of adventures in the course of which he was shipwrecked,
he tried to sail back to America. He was then taken by a French privateer,
and while in Brest was recognised by Tate, whom he had met in America
and who identified him as an American. He then joined the Irish Brigade

of the Republican service and found himself in Bantry Bay. He returned safely to France, and at first was going into the army of the Sambre and Meuse, but joined Tate's expedition instead. He then gave his version of the occupation of Trehowel, and the behaviour of the grenadiers. His adventures were not over, since he managed to escape from Portchester castle, a military prison of great antiquity, and disappeared, historically, for good.

Robert Morrison was a captain, aged thirty-five, and born in Bangor, County Down. When he was sixteen he became a servant of a number of gentlemen in France. When war broke out between Britain and France he said that he was forced to join the French army. After some time he found himself as part of Tate's force. He described the landing and how the only provisions they had were biscuits, cheese and brandy. He concluded that had he known the expedition was against England, 'he would not have entered into it, or have fought against his king and country'. The third officer, Captain Nicholas Tyrrell, was also thirty-five and was born near Dublin. When he was fifteen he went to stay with his aunt in France, and when the revolution broke out he was compelled to join the army. When he joined Tate he assumed they were bound for the West Indies and that, 'he knew nothing of being to land in Wales'. One oddity concerning Tyrrell is that a turnkey in ColdBath Fields said that, 'he verily believes the above named N Tyrrell has been seen by the Examinant at the Magpie and Stump, a recruiting House in Clerkenwell, about two years since, when he appeared to be acting as a recruiting Serjeant'. Many others had informed him that they had seen Tyrrell before.[101]

There was a curious complication about the identity of Tate. For some reason, which Lord Milford elevates to 'every reason', he believed that the commander of the invasion forces 'is an Englishman', in fact Governor Wall formerly governor of what is now Senegal. Having informed the duke of Portland of his suspicions on 24 February, Milford goes on to write: 'I shall have the Honor of writing your Grace by tomorrow's post when I shall be able to inform you whether Governor Wall is among the Prisoners knowing his person perfectly.'

This Wall had been the centre of a scandal in Senegal, because he had ordered such a severe flogging for a soldier that the man died. He then fled to the continent, but in 1797 returned to Britain, and he was eventually hanged for the offence.[102] The rumour seems to have spread, and clearly, in his day, Wall was a well known character. Thus, while escorting the officers to London, Cawdor reports that: 'At Uxbridge the rage of the mob was chiefly directed against Tate, who was supposed to be Wall, and he trembled almost to convulsions.'[103] This insistence upon Wall being present is another illustration of how quickly rumours were established, and how immoveable they were once they became part of the mythology. Two of the least accurate accounts actually named 'Governor Wall as second in command' to Tate,[104] and the other writes of 'Tate, and of the notorious Governor Wall, his coadjutor'.[105]

However, when Milford next wrote to Portland, he suggested that the commander was James Cockburn, who lost the West Indian island of St Eustatius to the French, and was court-martialled and cashiered. Finally Milford wrote again on 26 February: 'I have seen the Commander, who, from the description given of him by the first Prisoners that were taken, I had reason to believe him to have been Col. Wall, whose Person I well knew.'[106]

The most satisfactory explanation for these assumptions is that offered by Salmon. This is that Milford, having learned that the commander was not French, concluded that he must be British with a grievance against his country, 'and so thought of Wall and Cockburn'.[107]

Meanwhile, the rank and file French soldiers, having marched to Haverfordwest, arrived at one or two in the morning and were confined there. The main prison was in the castle, but this clearly could not cope with such numbers of prisoners although some 500 were lodged there. And so three parish churches, those of St Mary, St Thomas and St Martin as well as the Guildhall were marshalled to hold them. The churches were obviously unsuitable for holding prisoners. Apart from any other reason, they were doing considerable damage, especially to St Mary's. The bulk were therefore moved to the Golden prison in Pembroke, and the rest were kept in Haverfordwest castle.

So the latest batch of French prisoners entered the appalling maelstrom in which all prisoners of war find themselves; in the case of those of that period, it was a world of especial starvation, manipulation, and struggle for survival. The fond hope was for escape, and this soon became a profitable business for local people able to arrange it. Nor of course were the Pembrokeshire prisoners alone. By 1798 there were 35,000 French prisoners in Britain, and by 1814 this number had increased to 'upwards of seventy thousand'.[108] Many died, others learned and used skills which they employed in their community outside the prison since parole was common.

The conditions in the prisons of the time were, famously, extremely bad, and the pioneer prison reformer John Howard was indefatigable in his attempts to improve them. He managed to include in his massive series of inspections the prisons of even such a remote area as Pembrokeshire. His reports show that in Haverfordwest the prisons were as bad as any, and that the treatment of French and American prisoners in Pembroke captured in earlier conflicts, was worse than most. He visited in 1774, and again in 1782. The numbers had not changed much. In the county gaol in Haverfordwest in 1774 there were four debtors and one felon. In 1782 there were six debtors and no felons. In the town gaol, which was also the Bridewell, there were no prisoners in 1774 and in 1782 one debtor. When Howard visited in 1774, his report on the conditions was very like those he made on the hundreds of prisons he visited in those years: 'Six rooms. The two lowest are very damp dungeons: in one of these, as I was informed, a prisoner lost, first the use of his limbs, and then his life ... the upper rooms are dirty and offensive.'[109]

However, on his later visit, which was some fifteen years before the arrival of the French prisoners, a new gaol had been built within the castle. Now there were 'five cells and a kitchen for felons and a bride well room for men; and five rooms over them for debtors, and a room called the women's bridewell'.[110] But there was still a lot which could be improved: there was no infirmary or bath, the well was exposed, and a favourite with Howard: 'nor clauses against spirituous liquors hung up'.[111] There was also a small town gaol which Rutland later visited. In his opinion, which was not likely to be met charged sympathy for wrongdoers: 'The town gaol is a most terrible place, and really is not fit for the reception of the meanest criminals'.[112] Such prisons, not even the castle, could cope with the large number of French prisoners after the surrender.

When John Howard visited the prisons in Pembroke in 1779, he found there were fifty-six French prisoners in an old house adjoining to that in which the Americans were confined. His report demonstrates that these prisoners were in some of the worst conditions in Britain. In Deal for example, 'I had the pleasure of hearing the prisoners express their satisfaction'; at Chester 'they were healthy and well and made no complaints'. But in Pembroke: 'Most of them had no shoes or stockings, and some were also without shirts … They lay, in general, on the boards without straw … here was a court-yard, but no water or sewer.'

In the town gaol the prisoners, 'had some straw, but it not been changed for many weeks'.[113] Howard visited again in 1782 to discover a new prison and noted it, 'as dirty and offensive'. Some were confined to their room and kept on, 'short allowance' for making an escape. The former 'agent' had been dismissed.[114] Finally he noted: 'These prisons are usually guarded by the militia, and the sentinels have in several instances shewn themselves too ready to fire on the prisoners, in which they have been countenanced by the officers. Several persons have thus been killed on the spot.'[115]

The prospects did not look good for the invaders who were imprisoned since, in the eighteenth century, the fifteen years since Howard visited was not likely to see much improvement in prison conditions. Although Lord Milford, who does not claim to have visited, reported to Portland on 24 February that the prisoners were being well looked after:

> Mr. Mansell who will have the Honor of delivering this to your Grace is Commissary for the French Prisoners [Salmon notes that these were prisoners taken earlier in the war] in Pembroke under whose care they have experienced every indulgence & attention possible. He is a young man of infinite Skills in his Profession as a Surgeon & well worthy your Grace's protection.[116]

In Pembroke the prisoners were housed in something called the Golden Prison. Rutland, when he saw it as the prisoners were being moved, felt it was very insecure. But he notes that their treatment 'was such, as to satisfy them perfectly',[117] and that they were sorry to be going to Portsmouth where they suspected conditions would be much harder.

There also seems to have been established a hospital at a place called Barnlake. This is located near Burton and Neyland on the Haven. In a letter to Cawdor dated 20 March 1797, Colby gives first hand evidence of the fact, reported by Rutland, of the serious ill health of the prisoners:

> I postponed answering the letter you honoured me with till I should have the satisfaction of informing your lordship that the prisoners had sailed out

of the Harbour this morning – Had they been detained a fortnight longer I really think half of their numbers would have been in our Hospitals – near a hundred fell ill in the last week – 114 were carried into the Hospital at Barnlake yesterday. 28 are in the Hospital in this Town (Haverfordwest) – we have buried about 20 – the situation of those at Barnlake is miserable in the extreme. The chief disorder is Flux.[118]

So the effect of the arrival of hundreds of French prisoners to be housed, fed and given at least basic care can be imagined. It required considerable administrative skills, and of course posed huge problems of control. The difficulty of exerting such control is shown by a dramatic escape from Pembroke. Legend has it that the prisoners, with the help of two local women, managed to tunnel out of the prison. Since the 'two women' has become something of a linchpin of the story, the version set out by H.L. Williams, in which they first seem to be mentioned, should be dealt with first.[119] He writes that the women provided material such as bones for the prisoners 'curious workmanship'. They fell in love, precisely with the commissary and the engineer, and helped the tunnelling by carrying away all the material which was excavated. Twenty-five prisoners escaped, taking the women with them. The women 'were disguised in men's attire'. They captured a brig, and sailed to France. There the 'young women were united in marriage to their lovers, for whom they had dared so much'. The engineer and his wife returned to Britain (during the short peace of the Treaty of Amiens), and went to Merthyr. He worked in the mines, and 'they opened a large inn there'. Not only that, upon their return 'they gave the full particulars of their escape from the prison'. As soon as the war was renewed, 'they left Wales for France and have not since been heard of. Dr. Mansell of Pembroke posted handbills all over the kingdom offering a reward of 500 guineas for the recovery of the two young women, dead or alive'. Laws slightly embellishes the account which he copied from Williams. In his version Dr Mansell becomes, 'a leading man in Pembroke', the women are labelled 'traitorous', and despite this, 'it is to be hoped they lived happily ever afterwards'.[120]

In the matter of the women, it is worth dwelling upon the biography of one of the French officers. There are a number of reasons for this. The first is that he illustrates that not all the invaders were scum, or in Cawdor's phrase, 'stupid Paddies'. The second is that he was the centre of a rather romantic and human story, which for once is true. And thirdly, even when there is strong historical evidence to the contrary, myths have mysteriously risen about him, as about so much else. And he is anyway an interesting and somewhat characteristic revolutionary figure. His name was Pierre-Honoré Boudon de St Amans, not, as it is sometimes spelt, Amand.

He was born in 1774 in the chateau of St Amans, in the commune of Castelculier to the east of Agen. Agen is situated between Bordeaux and Toulouse, and is the capital of Lot-et Garonne. He became a professional soldier, serving as a sub-lieutenant in the Dragoons de la Republique. In 1793 he ran into his first taste of trouble, in what were very trying times. He lived in Paris with a friend, and without the latter knowing, he 'borrowed' some of his money. He promised to pay it back but did not, and his friend regarded this as theft. St Amans then turned to his friend's mistress to ask her to sort it out. However, his friend saw the two together in the street, and this was the last straw. His friend created a great fuss, a crowd assembled, and the Police Commissioner searched his home. The most dangerous thing imaginable was found there: a white cockade. This could easily have attracted a death sentence, since Robespierre and the Terror were still in power. As so often in his life, his luck changed. A distinguished doctor, a friend of the family, came to Paris and just managed to intervene. It was arranged that St Amans should be dispatched to Brest to work in the pharmacy of the military hospital.[121]

He was, of course, imprisoned after the Pembrokeshire invasion and at some point, probably whilst on parole, he began a relationship with a local woman of good family, Miss Anne Beach, described by Rutland as 'a lady of some fortune'. She was the sister-in-law of a well placed gentleman, Rev. James Thomas. At about the same time he held two prestigious positions in Haverfordwest: as headmaster of the grammar school, and as vicar of St Mary's, the most eminent of the parish churches. Not only was he an especially successful headmaster, but in 1811 he became the first clergyman to become mayor of Haverfordwest, an historic and much prized position.[122]

It is not clear exactly when St Amans and Beach married, but it was probably in 1802. Certainly they were married by 1802, the year of the Peace of Amiens because in that year his father travelled to Britain to meet his daughter-in-law. He was welcomed by the father of his daughter-in-law, Dominicus, a colonel in the East India Company, at the home

Above: 1 The Surrender.

Right: 2 John, Baron Cawdor, Commander of the defending forces.

3 Wolfe Tone, Irish patriot, and advocate of attacks on Ireland.

4 French prisoners in the 'hulks'.

A WELCH PEASANT AND HIS WIFE,
in their accustomed Habits, and with the kind of Weapons
that several Thousand People appeared with near Fishguard,
Feb:24. 1797. the Day the French surrendered to L.ᵈ Cawdor &
Colonel Colbey's Troops.   The wonderful Effect that the Scarlet
Flannel had that Day should never be forgotten.——
Lord Cawdor very Judiciously placed a considerable number of
of Women in that Drefs, in the rear of his Army, who being
considered by the French as regular Troops, contributed in no
small degree, to that happy, and unexpected, Surrender.——

5 'A Welch Peasant and his Wife': a source of evidence for the legend of the women in red flannel.

6 Tregwynt Manor: Where Colonel Knox received news of the attack.

7 Trehowel Farm. Seized and used as French Headquarters.

Above and below: 8 & 9 Llanwnda Church

10 Royal Oak, where the surrender was negotiated.

Above and below: 13, 14, 15 The churches of Haverfordwest St Mary's, St Martin's, and St Thomas'. The churches in Haverfordwest mobilised to hold French prisoners.

Opposite above: 11 The badge with 'Fishguard'.

Opposite below: 12 The uniforms of the regiment at the time that the honour was awarded.

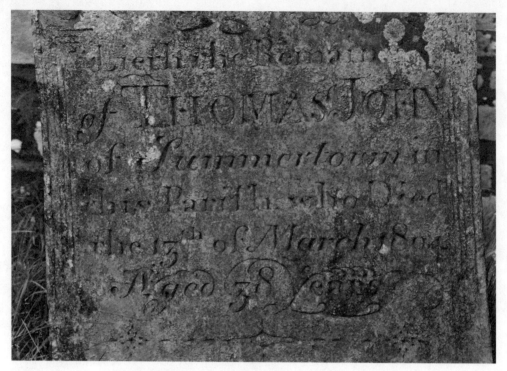

16 The gravestone of Thomas John, in the churchyard in Little Newcastle.

17 John, Duke of Rutland.

18 Jemima Nicholas, from the Fishguard Tapestry.

19 The ruins of Fishguard Fort.

of Sir Charles Greville.[123] Such hospitality was commonly offered to French gentlemen who had been captured, by British gentlemen: 'there were scores of country squires and gentlemen who treated the paroled officers as guests and friends, and who no doubt secretly rejoiced when they heard of their escapes.'[124]

In October 1804 the French government gave permission for St Amans to return to France.[125] In 1807 he again found himself in serious trouble. At a reception at Lagarde castle, the house silver disappeared and was found hidden in the park. St Amans and a servant were accused of the theft, and although he protested his innocence, in June he was imprisoned in Bordeaux. Although he was freed due to lack of evidence, a campaign of vilification began which led to his family asking that he and his wife be returned to Britain. This was impossible, and so internal 'exiles' of various kinds were suggested. He was finally freed in November of the same year, in part because his wife wrote an apparently very effective letter on his behalf. In January 1808 they went to Montpelier, and because of favourable reports from the prefect of Herault, supervision was lifted in September 1812.[126]

During his time in Pembrokeshire he apparently met some very distinguished people, amongst them Sir Charles Greville and Sir William Hamilton. Through such contacts he came to know the work of Wedgwood, and spent time studying pottery and ceramics. This led to a distinguished career in France, which was commemorated in a major exhibition of his work in Agen in 1968: 'Pierre-Honoré Boudon de Saint-Amans, Poteries, Sulfures'.

The central point which has been made about the events of the invasion is that all kinds of statements have been made which are either of doubtful veracity or quite untrue. And so we return to the place of myth making, in this case about St Amans. For example Kinross writes that St Amand [sic] and Miss Beach, together with her friend Eleanor Martin, were the agents of the escape from Golden prison in Pembroke. She allegedly brought in provisions, and in this way concealed large meat bones which enabled the prisoners to tunnel their way out via a 60ft tunnel. After this they stole a yacht belonging to Cawdor – a nice irony – and then captured a brig in which they sailed to St Malo.[127] He quotes as his source Edward Laws, *Little England beyond Wales*, but Laws does not mention any such allegation, although there *was* such an escape with all the attendant taking of craft.

The allegation of Miss Beach's involvement cannot be true. In the first place it would be very unlikely that a woman of the social standing of Miss Beach would engage in such menial work, or that she would collude in the escape of prisoners and then disappear. Unfortunately, such myths, especially if romantic, have a way of becoming enshrined as fact. Thus, in a very interesting French article substantially concerned with Amans' later career as an expert in ceramics (he was something of a pioneer in the field), and clearly drawing upon Kilross, the myth of his part in the escape is perpetuated.[128] More conclusive is the fact that the Duke of Rutland went to Pembroke with Cawdor on 20 August 1797 to see the prisoners embark for Portsmouth. He specifically mentions that Amans, or as he calls him Amand, 'of low grade' was amongst them, and that he and Miss Beach were betrothed.[129]

That there was an escape is not in doubt. Rutland describes how they then boarded a 'fine large pleasure boat',[130] ironically belonging to Cawdor. From there they boarded a coasting brig and, it is claimed, reached St Malo, and that some timbers were washed ashore from Cawdor's boat. And there is a letter from the officer responsible, dated 18 July 1797, with which anyone who has worked in a prison would sympathise:

> I am sorry to inform you that On Tuesday morning last [Salmon points out that this date was wrong] thirty one of the french Prisoners Effected their Escape (one of which number has been Retaken) by undermining throw the Prison wall Sixty feet beyond the furthest sentinel; Seazed a Small Boat with which they get off but the Violent storm of wind makes it impossible that they can Remain at sea; I have therefore sent three different Partys along the coast and make not the least doubt of their being all Retaken. I hope their Escape will not be Imputed to any neglect of mine as the Commissary as well as myself did all in Our Power to guard against such an unforeseen accident. Signed by Ensign Cole.[131]

In a scholarly analysis of the escape, Rose starts from the observation of Rutland that they (the French) originally brought over four women, but 'two of them made their escape in Lord Cawdor's pleasure boat'.[132]

They then boarded a sloop.[133] From there it is claimed they reached St Malo. It is known that in the French party there were four wives of the soldiers, who, it has been suggested were to do laundry. Although Rose has discovered, two of them were officers' wives, which raises a question as to the likelihood of them being laundresses. Rose gives their names, and traces the two officers' wives to the *Royal Oak* hulk in Portsmouth, whence they had accompanied their husbands when they were transferred there. One of the two officer's wives, Madame Grillere, gave birth to a child.[134]

Rose then turns to the matter of the enormous reward offered by Dr Mansell or Mansel. The critical fact here is that Mansell, who was a surgeon and had been the agent for the French prisoners, had been dismissed and replaced in April 1797, and therefore, was not the agent at the time of the escape. It follows that it would have been no concern of his to post a reward. If it happened at all, why did he and when? The explanation offered by Rose centres upon the activities of a French sailor called Jacques Debon and his commander, called Michel Dulaurent Dugué. Their ship was a privateer, and at the end of 1796 the ship was captured, taken to Milford Haven, and the men were imprisoned in Pembroke. At this time Mansell was still the agent, and it was he who reported on 18 January that thirty-two prisoners had escaped. Rose's contention is that Debon was amongst them, and since now a captain, he was captured at sea again on 21 June 1797. Rather remarkably, his ship was taken by William Dobbin (the revenue service was allowed to take privateers), who, it will be remembered, had been singled out by Cawdor for his contribution to the mustering of force against the French.

Although it seemed that the prison at Pembroke was full, Debon was again sent to Pembroke. Here he will have met the prisoners from Fishguard, and some fortnight later he escaped again. It was this escape which was the subject of Ensign Cole's letter. The agent who had succeeded Mansell wrote on 24 July that he, 'Observed that the Captain (Jacques Be Bon) [sic] of the L'Audacieux privateer, broke out of the prison in Pembroke some time back, and took a vessel belonging to Lord Cawdor, by which means he and about 30 more got safe to Brest.'[135] French sources reveal that Debon was an accomplished escapee, having previously escaped from Plymouth in 1793. Rose suggests that elements of the two escapes have become merged, and this appears a convincing suggestion, considering they were so close together; that they involved French prisoners; and that Debon was in both. As for the two women, Rutland is rarely wrong in what he reports: they could not have been French, and it follows that if they existed, even if separated from the detail which writers like Williams so remarkably provide, they must have been local.

The next purpose was to get rid of the prisoners. On 26 February, Cawdor wrote to Portland: 'it is my intention in a few days to order 120 Prisoners who have been confined for some time in a place of no security at Pembroke, to be put on board Ships I have directed Capt. Longcroft to have in readiness.'[136] Eventually, 'at Milford they embarked in three brigs and a Danish vessel which Captain Longcroft had taken up, and they sailed to Portsmouth under an escort of frigates whose senior officer had strict orders not to let the convoy out of his sight.'[137]

And so the prisoners were sent to the hulks. As places for the confinement of prisoners, these had become especially important since the advent of American independence. And they were to be a standard part of the penal system until the 1870s. The last hulk to be run was in Gibraltar and was closed in 1875. They were to become a familiar part of the penal system from the end of the eighteenth century onwards, and were legendary for both the corruption in their administration, and problems arising from the fact that often convicts worked with freemen, which led to trafficking. They were also dangerous and unhealthy places. One famous hulk the *Justitia* received its first convicts in March 1778 and 'out of six hundred and thirty two prisoners who had been received, one hundred and thirty six had died'.[138] As Rutland had observed, whatever conditions had been like for the prisoners in Pembrokeshire, the prospects in the hulks were grim indeed. The conditions for the prisoners of war were no better than those for ordinary prisoners, and may even have been worse. Complaints were incessant, and usually rejected. A French officer complained in 1816 that, 'Four hundred malefactors are the maximum of a ship appropriated to convicts. From eight hundred to twelve hundred is the ordinary number of prisoners of war, heaped together in a prison ship of the same rate.'[139] They did not even achieve their main aim, which was to keep prisoners secure: '*Vigilant* seems to have hardly deserved her name, for in the year 1810 alone no less than thirty two prisoners escaped from her, and of these only eight were recaptured.'[140]

The casualty numbers in the invasion are difficult to calculate precisely. The general consensus seems to be that perhaps three or four were killed on each side. This does not include the woman shot and killed by a local soldier. Nor does it include the eight French troops commonly agreed as having been killed during the landing. To these must be added the many French soldiers who died after capture. The local people who were killed, and for that matter wounded were all civilians. None of the local soldiers were killed or injured.

There are two further aspects of the history of the local troops which have been insufficiently recognised. The first is that they were noticeably inactive. Apart from some scouting, they did not try to engage the enemy at all. They did not, for example, seek out those who were spoliating the countryside, and stop them. Such fighting, and for that matter such dying and injury as happened, involved only the local peasants. Indeed, Rutland, who was accurate and sympathetic, observed that, 'Lord Cawdor disposed his men along the different heights in the neighbourhood of Fishguard and from what we could see they were never once within half a mile of the enemy.'[141]

There was some contact. For example, as I have written, Rose states that Cawdor and his staff had been to Pencaer, had watched soldiers plundering a farmhouse, and captured a French soldier who 'was so drunk & alarmed nothing could be obtained from him'.[142] It may be noted that that seems to have been no attempt, in this case as in others, to stop the looting. A Victorian writer, and an important contributor to legend, notes with pride how, 'The military now made their appearance ... the Castlemartin Yeomanry Cavalry, looking so smart in their richly embroidered uniforms and elegant trappings, that it was no wonder the French thought that they were all officers.'[143] However 'elegant' they may have looked, the attempt to invade Pembrokeshire failed without the local troops using their weapons, with the notable exception of one soldier who accidentally killed a local woman, Jones writes 'whilst loading a pistol in a public house'.[144] Reference is made to this incident in the report of the adjudicator who reported on claims by those who were injured: 'I have also sent an affidavit of the manner in which the poor woman at Fishguard, was killed by one of Lord Cawdor's Cavalry.'[145] More detail has been uncovered by Rose from an inquest held on 2 March 1797 into the death of the woman. Her name was Rebecca Bowen, and she received, 'one Mortal Wound a little Way below her Navel' ... on 28 February when a pistol held by a man named Filkin accidentally went off.[146]

There is a further curiosity which derives from this lack of engagement – that received history identifies the Pembrokeshire yeomanry as the victors. They actually did no more than the other units who were present: the Militia and the Volunteers. Yet the latter are generally eclipsed by the supposed role of the Yeomanry. The only explanations for this must be that Cawdor's unit was the Yeomanry; that Knox and by extension, his troops were subject to accusations of cowardice, as we shall see; and that while the Militia and the Volunteers were eventually disbanded, the Yeomanry, in various forms, survives until the present day.

Perhaps one of the most extraordinary events of the whole invasion story is this persisting glory accorded to the Pembrokeshire Yeomanry on this occasion. In 1853, when there seemed a possibility of trouble once again from the French, Queen Victoria underlined the performance of the Pembrokeshire Yeomanry, by granting a request from the regiment to be given the privilege of putting *Fishguard* as a battle honour on its standards and insignia, the only regiment ever to have been awarded such an honour for a conflict on British soil. And surely the only battle honour to be accorded to a regiment which neither fired a shot, nor as far as is recorded, killed one of the enemy. There must be a question as to why the defenders were not sent in to engage the invaders when the latter were terrorising the local people. A perfectly logical answer, especially when the social conditions and the perceptions of the officers as to the loyalty of their troops are taken into account, is that Cawdor was not sure that they could be trusted to fight.

To identify this as historical fact is in no way to demean the subsequent honour that the regiment attained. Their enthusiasm is demonstrated by their willingness, when ordered to be disbanded in 1828, to continue to serve without pay and allowances. They were restored to the payroll in 1831.[147] The regiment later served in the Boer War, where a sergeant was recommended posthumously for the Victoria Cross. The regiment went on to serve in both world wars, and has since been a part of the Territorial Army.[148] But none of this honourable history has anything to do with the invasion of 1797.

Nothing has soured the story of the invasion as much as its aftermath. And nothing has confused writers so much as trying on the one hand to maintain the celebration of victory and on the other to offer some rational explanation of what followed. These are the matters to be dealt with in the next chapter.

4

The Aftermath:
Cowardice and Treason?

It is a matter of accepted fact that one of the characteristics of the Welsh gentry, in the eighteenth century in particular, was a lack of concern in public affairs, except for purposes of self service and betterment. This extraordinary apathy seems to have been a prevailing characteristic of Welsh members of Parliament, since there is documentary evidence of their idleness, and it was in their dereliction that it found its highest expression. Examples are easy to find. Sir William Owen, a Pembrokeshire member from 1722 to 1774, and John Symmons, another Pembrokeshire representative from 1746 to 1761, not only never held an office, but they never spoke in the House.[1] If it is possible, a member for Haverfordwest from 1747 to 1784, a period of nearly forty years, was even worse. William Edwardes, 'gives the impression of creeping sclerosis: he never spoke in the house, never begged for any favour or office, and never voted against a single government after 1760'.[2] In an unforgettable summary, Geraint Jones states that 'Welsh members of Parliament … have few claims upon the curiosity of posterity'.[3] William Knox, the father, was quite unlike these and other landowners. He established the first Pembrokeshire Agricultural Society, the first post office and market in Fishguard, and set up a packet service between Milford and Waterford. His:

> Piety and sensibility, who in the genuine spirit of a christian, not waiting for the lingering produce of a subscription, genuinely instituted one [a Sunday School] at his own expense, under proper superintendants, and without restriction as to number of scholars. From the novelty of such a school, and on an account of a donation of books, &c. with which this opening was attended, it was croudedly [sic] resorted to.[4]

Although allegedly ill-tempered, argumentative, and bitter about the government's failure to compensate him for land losses in America, or to reward him properly, nevertheless, in short: 'intellectually he was far ahead of anyone else in the county'.[5] We saw earlier though, that because of his enclosing of land, he was described as an 'Irish wolf'.

But they *were*, by the standards of the day and indeed by our day, *noveaux riche*, and father must have been the object of envy because he took the initiative when the rest were doing so little. One may reasonably surmise that such activities, together with the fact that he was an Irishman, would be unlikely to make him popular in a county and a district where apathy, and complacency, were characteristic of the gentry.

Knox junior had been the centre of allegations before the invasion. It was alleged that his troops had helped with the seizure of a cargo at Fishguard, an allegation which he strongly denied. In a letter he wrote on 29 December 1795, he stated 'that Fishguard and its neighbourhood are in a state of perfect tranquillity and have been ever since the 5th instance'. It would appear that as part of a protest, the rudder was removed from a ship. But, 'the rudder was taken off at the recommendation of the Magistrates with the consent of the owners present and of the Master who even directed the people how to do it'. He goes on to say:

> I have seen no appearance of a riot. I was not in Fishguard on the 5th instant but two of my officers who were there, have assured me, the men of the Corps who were then in Fishguard ... behaved perfectly contrary to the Collector's statement ... the Corps was not assembled that day, it was not a day of exercise, nor did the Magistrates apply for their assistance.[6]

His denial was supported by Gwinfardd Dyfed, writing in the *Cambrian Register* for 1795:

> At a time of impending famine, in consequence of those confederated bloodsuckers attempting to whip of a cargo of corn and butter, with its destination strongly suspected, a number of poor labourers and peasants of this and the adjoining parishes instigated by actual want, and the unsatisfied clamour of their children and families, met to remonstrate in the most moving and peaceable manner with the enemy of their species.

Not only did the 'enemies' claim that this was a riot, but they went on to fabricate allegations against, 'the commanding officer of the 'fencibles', [not in fact Knox, but clearly one of his officers] who attended most humanely on the occasion, from a wish to mediate between the parties, and satisfy both, with as little violence as possible to either.'[7]

For his part in the invasion, as we will go on to see, Knox duly received the thanks of several county bodies. And he received thanks from much more eminent sources. On 1 March 1797, the Duke of Portland wrote that having placed a letter Knox had written before the King, the latter had commanded him to express his entire satisfaction at the zeal and alacrity which were shown by the Fishguard volunteers on the late descent of the French in Pembrokeshire. 'He will always recollect, with particular pleasure, the striking manner in which these two valuable qualities (attachment and bravery) distinguish the character of the Fishguard Volunteers'.[8]

In the same month, March 1797, Thomas Knox received a visit from a messenger with the news that a regular army officer, Major Williamson, had been sent by General Rooke 'to examine into his conduct, in consequence of charges of a most serious nature having been alledged [sic] against him'.[9] The next day, 22 March, Knox met Williamson in Haverfordwest and was shown a letter written by someone called M'Namara who, it emerged, was a very rich landowner in Breconshire; had been a member of Parliament; was High Sheriff of that county; and had been colonel of a regiment of Volunteers. In all, a powerful and influential figure, who had been enlisted as an ally by Hassall. His letter contained a letter from the latter, and Knox was allowed to read it. It was serious and damning.

Before discussing the letter and its consequences, it will be useful to be reminded about Charles Hassall's background. Like the Knox family, he was of Irish birth, and wrote two very forward looking and expert reports for the government on agriculture in Pembrokeshire and Carmarthenshire respectively. He was himself a respected and successful farmer in Pembrokeshire at Eastwood, near Narbeth. At one point in his life, he might have made some slight difference to the course of history, since he shot Lieutenant General Sir Thomas Picton, a Pembrokeshire man, in the throat during a duel. Picton had a distinguished military and administrative career, at various times being the governor of several islands in the West Indies, although he was charged and convicted of allowing a female prisoner to be tortured, a conviction which was overturned. It has been said that 'he rendered brilliant service' in the Peninsular war.[10] He was killed at Waterloo.

Of especial relevance to the understanding of Hassall's pursuit of Thomas Knox is the fact that he had been the land steward of William Knox's estate at Llanstinan, and had been dismissed. His elder brother Thomas was also very successful. He had a farm called Kil Rhiwau (variously spelt) in north Pembrokeshire. He was such a prominent figure that in about 1802 he got a 'premium' from the Society for the Encouragement of Arts for reclaiming about 1,000 acres 'of high uplands that might with sufficient propriety be termed *mountains*.'[11] The Hassall brothers had clearly made a mark in Pembrokeshire, and Charles was about to make another.

In his letter Hassall began by claiming that the governor of Fishguard fort, 'complains aloud of the cowardly conduct of Col. Knox, who ran away with his men the morning of the day after the French landed', and that he ordered that the guns of the fort be spiked. The gunners refused 'and swore they never saw nor never heard of such cowardly conduct in their lives':

> indeed Col. Knox's officers and men were loud in their declarations of the contempt they held him in. I was the first who stopped them on the road in their retreat, and the men expressed themselves much provoked in having been compelled to retreat ... but the young gentleman thought it more prudent to provide for the safety of himself, and abandon the town and neighbourhood to their fears and their foes.[12]

In passing, it may be noted, that although Hassall may have heard some remarks of the kind, this claim is inconsistent with the reaction of his troops which is described below.

Another very condemnatory letter had been sent to the War Office. Dated 3 March 1797, its authorship is in some doubt, but the ferocity of his view is not. Writing of Fishguard fort:

> Instead of protection it might have proved our ruin. For on the Enemy's first debarcaton, our worthy Governor [Salmon notes that he means Knox] was missing, and was neither seen, nor heard of, until they laid down their arms.

The Fort was abandoned, and his brave Garrison (the like troops the world never saw) were found straying in Trefgarne forest, the next day at noon, where possibly they might have wandered as long as the Israelites did in the Wilderness, had not the Pembrokeshire fencibles luckily picked them up on their march from Haverfordwest to Fishguard.[13]

Knox's response was swift and firm. On 22 March he wrote to General Rooke asking for a court martial 'as soon as possible'. Rooke replied on 2 April. His letter was one of several which were wildly contradictory. It read that: 'It is his Royal Highness's opinion, that no general court-martial can be granted for your trial, as volunteer corps are not subject to martial laws, *except during the existence of an actual invasion.*' [My italics.][14] The next tactic was to ask for a Court of Enquiry. The only letter which Salmon was able to identify as any kind of response was another strange contradictory letter, this time from Lord Milford: 'I am sorry to be under the necessity of signifying to you his Majesty's wish that you would resign your command of the Fishguard Fencibles. *His Majesty is, however, perfectly well satisfied with your conduct, courage, and loyalty, shewn on a late occasion.*' [my italics][15]

A later letter dated 24 May 1797 from Portland to Milford, continues the curious ambivalence. Acknowledging Knox's resignation as Commanding Officer, the duke goes on to direct that Knox be told that: 'His Majesty, in accepting the resignation, was at the same time graciously pleased to express himself perfectly satisfied with the proofs of courage and loyalty Mr. Knox has always manifested in his Majesty's service.'[16] It is as though the authorities wished that they had never been persuaded to start the proceedings in the first place, and now wished to drop the matter.

In the light of the very serious charges against him, the content of such letters must have left Knox bemused, as indeed they do the modern reader. But his resolve was not weakened. He now set in motion, 'measures ... for instituting a prosecution in the Court of King's bench, against Mr. Charles Hassall for defamation'. Again he was thwarted, because to proceed he needed the letters written by Hassall and M'Namara, but the Duke of York 'did not think himself at liberty to give them.'[17] On 15 April a number of officers (not from the Fishguard Volunteers) wrote to Rooke:

We think it our duty to apprize you that the regard we feel for our repu-tations as officers must force us into the painful necessity of resigning the

Commissions we have at present the honor to hold rather than under any circumstances risk our characters by acting under the command of Lieut-Col. Knox, whose ignorance of his Duty & want of judgement must be fully known to you.

Amongst others, it was signed by Cawdor (at the head), and Dudley and James Ackland. It was not until 2 May that Knox was made aware of this letter, and on 18 May, after having told Cawdor of his resignation as Commanding Officer of the Fishguards, he demanded to see a copy. Cawdor's reply was that he could, 'not transmit to you a copy of the letter you allude to with the signatures, without the permission of the officers whose names are affixed to it'.[18] But in the same letter he confessed that he had decided, 'to resign my commission rather than risk my character as an officer by serving under your command, viz., my conviction of your inexperience and ignorance of your duty, joined to want of judgement'. To this Knox replied on 23 May in the only terms left to a gentleman at the end of the eighteenth century. He informed Cawdor that this letter, 'make it incumbent upon me to call upon you for satisfaction. I leave it to your lordship to appoint time and place of meeting'. On the same day Cawdor replied that, 'I shall be ready to meet you at twelve o'clock to-morrow upon the turnpike road between Pembroke Ferry and the road that turns off to Williamston'.[19] It is considered doubtful if this duel ever took place, or if not why not. There is no record that it did, or of any injury. There is though an entry in Cawdor's diary which indicates that he did meet Knox on the Williamston road on 24 May, the day requested for the duel: 'A very fine day. After breakfast rode to the Ferry. Met Joe there [Jos. Adams, his second, and one of the signatories to the refusal to serve under Knox] and Mr. Knox and Col. Vaughan near the Williamston road. Rode home alone back by ½ past one.'[20]

In the midst of all of this there appears a report to General Rooke by Colby, one of the most experienced of all the officers and, it will be remembered, an anchorman when the news came of the landing. Indeed he had recommended, in response to a request from the Mayor of Haverfordwest, the steps to be taken. These proved to be sound, and he concluded by riding to Fishguard to learn of the position on the ground. When he arrived he gave advice to Knox, which included sending in scouts in civilian clothes, and that:

During the time he conversed with Lt. Col. K'x in the Fort he appeared perfectly collected nor did Lt. Col. Knox shew any signs of timidity but on the contrary recollects in conversing with him that he intimated as if he intended to move out to the attack the enemy when his Newport Division had joined him.

He was surprised that Knox and his men had moved so far away from Fishguard, and 'asked him if the Enemy had appeared in such a force as to justify it. Does not recollect what answer he made him. But recollects his saying that the Enemy were then in possession of Fishguard'.[21] Stuart Jones went to the trouble of checking the (actual) authenticity of this document in the private papers of the Colby family.[22]

A new element now appeared. It was claimed in a letter of 31 March from Joseph Adams of Bristol, that some of the allegations against Knox emanated from Governor Vaughan of Fishguard, 'who held this language in strong terms to Mr. Chas. Hassall'. It had been alleged that Knox had ordered the guns, 'to be spiked, the ammunition to be destroyed, with running away fro thence, & with *cowardice*.' [His italics.] The writer Joseph Adams goes on, that Major Williamson:'examined many Officers & Gents who all declare they think Lt. Col. Knox leaving Fishguard proceeded from want of judgement & not from *cowardice* [his italics], that Genl. [Governor] Vaughan eats his words, and hath written a friendly letter to Lt. Col. Knox.'[23]

Governor Vaughan, whose conduct was not beyond reproach,[24] and who was a neighbour of the Knox family, wrote to Thomas Knox:

> I find that Hassall has been writing a pack of stuff to Mr. MacNamara, and he,
> I find has been telling the Duke of York who has sent down to Gen. Rooke
> orders to enquire into all our conduct during the time the French were here.
> I give you this hint that you may ask Colby when you see him as to particulars.[25]

Then, suddenly on 24 March the military secretary to the Duke of York wrote to Rooke to tell him that the duke was content with Knox's behaviour, and that the matter was finished.

For the Knox family however, the matter was far from finished. William Knox had been a very senior officer in the government, and he was not prepared to suffer such an attack on the reputation of his family. He therefore moved to London, the better to be able to take on those who had insulted his son. He wrote to the Under-Secretary of

State demanding a Board of Enquiry, which should be held in public, 'to vindicate the conduct of an Officer and a Corps to whom his Grace had signified in terms of high praise His Majesty's approbation'.[26] He wrote a long letter to the Under-Secretary, King, on 21 August, in which he pointed out that the proposed action against Hassall could not proceed unless his son had access to the several letters and reports which had been written.[27] After waiting several months for a reply, William wrote again, only to be told that he could not have copies of official correspondence. Dealing with M'Namara and Hassall proved equally frustrating, since they variously denied the existence of letters, or refused to confirm a version of Hassall's letter, an extract of which Thomas had taken at the time Williamson and Knox met in Haverfordwest. An odd compensation was offered to Knox, which was an invitation to a duel by M'Namara. The Knox lawyers then advised that there was no point in proceeding further, and the case was dropped.

Returning to the allegations that his men were disgusted by his behaviour, this was largely discredited when ten of his officers signed a memorandum supporting him:

> We the undersigned, now or late officers in the corps of Fishguard Volunteers, lately commanded by Lieut. Col. Knox, do declare, that we never said we held him in contempt, as we have been informed Mr. Charles Hassall reported we did, at the time of the French invasion; neither did we at that, or any other time, hear any of the men of the said corps express such sentiments; and we further declare, that we ever respected Col. Knox, in his character, as our Commanding Officer, and a gentleman, and that to the best of our judgement and belief, he acted, during the time of the said invasion, with the utmost spirit and good conduct.
> Dated Oct. 3rd, 1797.[28]

This is surely strong testimony of Knox's worth.

As proof that the officers were reflecting the views of the ordinary soldiers, when the unit next paraded after Knox's resignation, they mutinied and refused to take up their arms. Colonel Colby, now in military charge of Pembrokeshire and accountable to Rooke, ordered Major Bowen to fall the men in. It may be noted that Bowen had been one of the officers signing the note of support for Knox. Nothing would persuade the men to pick up their arms and Colby, having harangued them

to no effect, was forced to listen to them while they told him that they
had sworn loyalty to Knox. Colby advised them to disperse, and consider
their actions. But an important influence for calm was Knox himself,
who was present, and tried to persuade them that loyalty to him could
best be demonstrated by obeying the orders of their officers.[29] Eventually
the men calmed down, even agreeing to a proposal from London that
they would serve outside their home area in the event of invasion.[30]

Theories about the dire character of Knox did not end with his disgrace and death. One of the most bizarre ones suggests that he was in
league with the invaders since, according to this outlandish theory the
invasion was designed to re-establish Roman Catholic authority in
Britain. It has been suggested as recently as the late twentieth century
that St Leger, being an Irish Catholic, was deputed to meet Knox by
Tate, another Irish Catholic. Why, the question is asked, did Knox go
towards Trehowel, and not to the vantage point of Garn Fawr? Even
though in travelling from Tregwynt to Trehowel, Knox must have passed
Garn Fawr. And why did he give the order for the guns of the fort to be
spiked? This allegation goes on:

> Barry St. Leger met Thomas Knox at the gate of Trehowel and ordered him
> to make haste for Fishguard and get the guns of the Fort put out of action.
> The reason must have been given as soon as the landing was complete at
> Carreg Gwastad the Flotilla was to sail for Dublin Roads immediately after
> the Flotilla had captured the port of Lower Town [Fishguard] to be their port
> for further disembarkation.[31]

The highly questionable nature of such assumptions is demonstrated
by the absence of any evidence that the Knoxs were Roman Catholic.
On the contrary, William claimed descent from the Scottish reformer
John Knox, and, another son, John William was the Anglican rector of
Yerbeston in Pembrokeshire for fifty-two years,[32] while Thomas was
closely associated with Slebech church, near Minwear.

To put this fantasy into its morbid anti-Catholic context, note should
be taken that, as was pointed out earlier, Mortimer himself is accused of
being a collaborator:

> The owner of Trehowel farm was certainly not a Welsh Baptist. The origin of
> the name Mortimer was 'Mortimer' (Seine Maritime). Further possibilities

of connections with the French being: Mort meaning death, and Mere [sic] meaning the sea ... who did he marry? Was she a Maria, Theresa or a Brigid perhaps?[33]

Walter also suggests that the reason the invaders, *inter alia*, burnt the records in Llanwnda church was to destroy the suspicious nature of Mortimer's ancestry.[34]

There are several possible explanations for the pursuit of Knox. The first is that his motive in leaving Fishguard was cowardly. This would be very difficult to sustain, since he was not properly able to assess the size of the French force; and in the light of the evidence of Colby quoted above. In fact he underestimated its size, as we have seen, and had he attacked at that point in the event his force would have been slaughtered. Much more likely is the determination by Hassall, an exceptionally clever and resourceful man, to settle the score with the family. This determination would have been well received by the gentry because of the envy of many; of the superior quality of the Knox family; and their sudden rise to prominence in local society. That snobbery played a significant part, as might be expected, which is apparent in a letter from Charles Greville, an important figure in the foundation of the town of Milford, to Lady Cawdor: 'as to Knox, the old one says he is driven out of the country but he will make one more trial of being something from his chateau of Minner (Minwear)'.[35]

Whatever his enemies may have said about Thomas Knox, one final point needs to be made as evidence not only of their malice, but their hypocrisy - that although he did not attack the French at once, neither did any of the other defenders, at any time. The outcome in the event was that Hassall had his revenge, and the collusion with his vindictive campaign by so many of the influential stratum of Pembrokeshire society is a disgrace to their memory, and is long overdue being recognised as such.

In the years after the fracas William Knox seems to have remained a person of some position. In 1802 he was appointed Crown Agent for Prince Edward Island in 1801, and despite evidence of his contacts with the Prince of Wales (they exchanged gifts on St David's day in 1810), his personal fortune began to diminish, in part because of the extravagance of his son. At this time William was about seventy-eight. Remarkably, Thomas became a JP for Pembrokeshire, was given the freedom of

Haverfordwest, and settled into the life of a country squire at Minwear, but then slowly became insane. He apparently believed that he was a military expert and 'compared himself to Napoleon'. He engaged in a disastrous love affair, was almost sent to prison, and eventually died in poverty, and in isolation, 'probably in London, either in 1824 or 1825'.[36] Jones recounts how he spent a lot of time sorting out the last days of Thomas, and the possibility that he was in the East India Company, since a contemporary with the same name worked there. But he concludes that they were different people.[37]

There were others, of more humble origin, who were caught up in the recriminatory mood which seems to have been a feature of Pembrokeshire life after the invasion. One of those suspected of treason was Thomas Williams of Caerlem. He had guided the two French officers into Fishguard with the offer to surrender. But he was also the man whose wife had been raped and shot, so it is difficult to imagine that he was in league with the invaders. The farmer William Thomas, who had been robbed of his watch and buckles, was also suspected. Both were, however, released, Jones opines 'when it was learnt that they were churchmen'.[38] It should be stated at the outset that the received, and standard belief about these arrests and trials, is that they were anti-nonconformist measures, pursued with no justification at all. It is this deep rooted perception that will now be examined.

Others who were under suspicion were John Reynolds, a Baptist minister of a chapel near Solva, over a periodical which was 'probably one of the advanced type of publication,' whose house was searched.[39] Also arrested in connection with a periodical was a merchant from Haverfordwest called John Thomas, who is almost certainly Thomas, 'the shopkeeper in this town', whom Colby writes about to Cawdor, 'you ordered Capt. Ackland to take up and confine in the Prison under military guard'. He goes on to admonish Cawdor that there was no legal authority for this action. Colby advised Cawdor to regularise the position by recourse to a magistrate, to prevent 'proceeding at Law against your Lordship which the whole sect of Anabaptists say they are determined lads.' (sic.)[40] Another minister, Henry Davies of Llangloffan was investigated, and though not charged was submitted to a familiar eighteenth-century measure of disapproval by being burned in effigy at Fishguard fair.[41] When all preliminaries were over, three men were sent to prison for trial: John Reed, a weaver, who lived near Pencaer, very near to the French camp; Thomas John from Little Newcastle, a yeoman farmer; and Samuel Griffith of Poyntz Castle near Solva, also described as a yeoman farmer. All three were non-conformists.

After examination by magistrates, the three appeared at the Great Sessions in the Guildhall, Haverfordwest, on 11 April 1797. This was an appearance before a Grand Jury, which was to decide if a 'true bill' could be made out. The Grand Jury system has long been abolished in Britain, because it was likely to prejudice the final outcome of the case. John appeared first. He was charged, in essence, of visiting the enemy, giving them information as to the strength of the local force, and exaggerating the latter's weakness. He also allegedly encouraged the French to fight. Formally he was charged that he:

> Not regarding the Duty of his allegiance nor having the Fear of God in his Heart and being moved and seduced by the instigation of the Devil as a false Traitor did counsel comfort encourage and abet the said army in their said Enterprise and invasion of this kingdom and did give to the same army advice and information of and concerning the numbers arms strength and Discipline of the Troops of our said Lord the King.[42]

The charges against Griffith were similar, adding that he 'there joined himself to the said last mentioned Frenchmen and other Persons', mention of the latter clearly indicating that there were more locals involved. The Grand Jury decided that there was a 'true bill', and that two men, John, and Griffith, should be tried for high treason at the next Great Sessions, some six months ahead.

Events now seemingly took a dramatic turn, and were recorded at the time, probably by a Dr William Richards of Lynn, who was a native of Pembrokeshire, in a pamphlet entitled *Cwyn y Cystuddiedig*, (the complaint of the afflicted), which was published in 1798. It is interesting, in the light of earlier discussion, that this pamphlet was written in Welsh. It records that one of the principal witnesses against the two, an American serving with the French called Charles Prudhomme, made a statement which was witnessed, in which he claimed that he had not seen John in the French camp, that he had been promised money to say he had, and that he had briefed other Frenchmen, who also had not seen him, as to what they should say. He had pointed out to the gentlemen, 'the man I saw in the camp, but they would not believe me'. He later sent a note to

John specifying that he had been promised a total of sixty guineas if he gave false evidence. The only slightly suspicious thing he reported was that when he saw John on the road, he asked him if he was a servant of the King, and he replied 'no' - an inexplicable reply. Sergeant Major Binet also stated that the French prisoners had been bribed.

Reed had been bailed and the case against him dropped. But John and Griffith spent several months in prison waiting for trial. Despite Prudhomme's retraction, this took place on 7 September 1797 in Haverfordwest, with 126 potential jurors having been summoned, and the appearance of an array of very distinguished lawyers including, 'for the defence two of the leading barristers of the day, Mills and Blackstone'.[43] But the French witnesses variously refused to take the oath, refused to give evidence, and refused to acknowledge their statements. *The Times* reported of Prudhomme: 'To repeated remonstrances from the Bar and from the Bench, he could only be prevailed upon to answer, that if the French prisoners would speak, he would do so too. The Court ordered him back into close confinement, regretting that they had no further power at present over him'. This refusal, together with the refusal of others, led to the court agreeing with the prosecution that the witnesses, 'Had been tampered with, and reprobated the conduct of the gaoler for permitting such practices, recommending to the Sheriff to discharge him from his office'.

John had thirty-five witnesses on hand including two Welsh sailors, captured and held in the French camp. They were ready to say that they had not seen John there. The prosecution then abandoned their case, but the judge, as judges often do, felt that he should make his views plain. He admonished John to watch his behaviour, that there were many disloyal people about, and that they should be eliminated. The jury should acquit the prisoner, although he was not convinced of his innocence, 'regretting that justice appeared to have been defeated by the practices above alluded to'.[44]

When Griffith was put up, one witness Francois L'Hanhard, *Aide-de-Camp* to Tate, said that he had been seen in the French camp, but the prosecution felt that the case could not be sustained, so it did not call the two Rees cousins, local men, who were due to bear witness to Griffith's alleged sympathy with the French. So what was the evidence against the men?[45]

Six of the invasion force initially gave statements about the alleged activities of Thomas John in March 1797. They were Francois L'Hanhard;

Charles Prudhomme, an American sailor; Corporal Gaspard Dégouy; Private Pierre Maltbé; two grenadiers: Francois Ashet and Claude Meillé. Prudhomme's evidence was damning. He said that John had arrived in the French camp at 9 or 10 a.m., and he was told to ask John about the local forces. John said that there were 'not above two hundred soldiers', in Fishguard, and 500 in Haverfordwest. There were, 'only two cannons in the fort'. John advised them not to be afraid 'because all the Soldiers in this country had had no battles and would shoot one another: that the soldiers would only stand a quarter of an hour and then the country people to the amount of six hundred would be all for them'. John then returned to 'five or six Englishmen who came with him'. He came back later and said that 'there were only three hundred below'. His answer to an observation that there seemed to be many more was that 'half were women with red flannels'. Later, upon learning that the French were going to surrender, he said, 'there are a great many to give you help if you want to tell your friends of this' … and that several men with the army were without arms. There were three or four others with him. Prudhomme was warned to be sure he had identified the right man otherwise, 'he would have no reward for convicting any man'. Although they presented another man for identification, he said that was not the man he had seen.

Meillé stated that he saw John in the camp, and the latter went to the General *en seconde* (le Brun), who gave him a glass of brandy, and took him to the Commander-in-Chief, 'who talked a great deal with him at least three quarters of an hour'. Stuart Jones, in his massive support for the innocence of those charged, claims: 'incidentally John was a temperance man'.[46] It is not clear how he knows this: it is in any case certain that there is no necessary correlation between religious persuasion and taking alcohol. He returned at 1 p.m., and he was 'told to let him pass as he was going to the General'. L'Hanhard said he was ordered by Le Brun to give John a glass of brandy. But the most interesting statement was that John had been riding a bay horse with distinctive cropped ears. The two grenadiers saw the horse, one adding that he 'noticed the horse much', and recognised it when it was produced. L'Hanhard also recognised the bay, while Dégouy saw John mount the same horse.

John made a rambling statement, in which he denied having been to the camp. He and another man had been fired on by the French. He had been spying on them, and a Mr Propert asked him how many French there were, and he had told him about 200. When the French surrendered, Cawdor had asked for volunteers to go to the camp and bring up stragglers, and he volunteered. Cawdor though, according to *The Times*, pointed out at the trial that, 'The Prisoner had not been desired by him to bring up a Division of the French army on the day of the surrender, as he had pretended before the Magistrates.'[47]

Naturally, the notion of pretence was extremely damaging. In fact, there seems to have been a call for volunteers, and it seems to have been Ackland who made it. This is especially relevant, because Cawdor's statement further added to the undermining of the credibility of the defendant. It is, of course, possible that he confused Cawdor and Ackland at the time, or when he gave his statement. John talked to the prisoners, one of whom asked if they were in Ireland; another gave him his cutlass; and another asked if there was brandy or porter in town. A local man observed: 'you had some office with them too', to which he replied: 'no office, only Lord Cawdor sent me down to call them up'. He made no mention of a horse in his defence statement, except to say that he had lent his mare to Thomas Jenkins, for the use of Mr Bowen, a 'Fencible' officer.

L'Hanhard said that he had seen Thomas Davies, of Castle Villia (Willia), in the camp with Griffith. In his statement Davies said that he went, in company with a number of men, including Griffith to see what was happening. They saw eight or ten Frenchmen nearby, and called to some country people to help them capture the soldiers. They set out to do this, but the soldiers ran away. 'A great Many French' then appeared and led his horse to Trehowel, along with Griffith. Asked what his business was with the General, he replied none. He was taken to Tate, who asked him if he was from the English army, to which he replied that there had been a mistake. Tate gave them a safe escort out of Trehowel. The case against Davies was not pursued.

L'Hanhard also testified against Samuel Griffith of Poyntz Castle. He claimed that he saw him at about 10 or 11 a.m. on 23 March, in the company of French officers. He saw him again on the following Monday with Thomas Davies. These two parted, and the witness spoke to Griffith, who told him there were not many troops in the town, and the witness said '"you need not be afraid" because they came to fraternize with them'. Griffith said he knew that. Captain Pierre Bertrand was not quite so definite in his identification. On the same day at about 9 a.m. he 'saw a person in size and person a good deal like the man now shewn ... [but he thinks the beard was rather darker] in the French camp talking to L'Hanhard. He was wearing clothes 'similar to the dress now worn' by Griffith. He also saw him on the following Monday dismount and talk to L'Hanhard.

Then there appeared a rather surprising pair of witnesses. These were James and John Rees, who were cousins. They were local men, John being from St David's, and James from Haverfordwest. James said that he went to Pencairn (Pen Caer) Rock, near the French camp, where he saw Griffith 'in the midst of a great crowd of country people'. He heard him say that the 'French had not come there to do them any harm', where-upon his cousin charged Griffith with 'being of their party'. Griffith said that he would fight for his king while he had life, and 'that high words had passed between Griffith and his cousin John Rees'.

John Rees explained that he expected, 'to hear some person reply: [he] waited for some time but nobody answered, [and] being pro-voked at Griffith hold such language', argued with him. The ubiquitous Prudhomme now added that the day after the invasion he saw Griffith ride down to Trehowel House, and go inside.

On 18 March, Griffith made a statement. This was a long account of how he went to the high rock above Carn y Coch, 'where they saw about fifty or sixty men very few armed but some had pikes and some sticks'. Then about twenty-five or thirty Frenchmen came run-ning towards him and the French started 'delivering their muskets to the country people'. It is not clear, but of considerable significance, whether or not this was a feature of surrender or an implementation of the grand plan to subvert and convert local people. We shall go on to see that, whatever the motive, the authorities made every effort to retrieve the arms, thus and in other ways, procured by local people. When Griffith tried to take a musket, 'the Frenchman twisted it ... and made a push at him with his bayonet' very near his chest. There seemed, he went on, 'to be a confusion amongst the French', and he and Davies were seized and taken to see the General. Because of his English, Griffith asked him what 'countryman' he was and he replied that he was American. The General ordered an escort for them. Griffith then, 'had some words with one Rees [one of the cousins] of Arglwd [St David's]', and then went to watch the surrender.

So why were these people made to face such serious charges? In the case of such common people there are several possible reasons. The first is that they were innocent, and were hounded only because they were non-conformists. This has always been advanced as the reason, and in support of this it is pointed out that only non-conformists were charged. And so this is the commonly accepted explanation. This fits well with the mood of the time expressed, for example, by the Duke of Rutland and Colonel Colby. The duke, on his visit to Haverfordwest castle:

> paid a visit to the state criminals, one of whom [an Anabaptist] seemed as desperate and determined a villain as ever was seen ... it was the general opinion that they would not be hanged ... This part of the country is very much under the influence of the pernicious doctrines of Methodism ... these people are like wolves dispersed over the country. They are deceitful in their manners and, under the mask of religion, with piety and meekness in their mouths, they are pests to the community.[48]

Colby, in a letter written to Cawdor on 20 March 1797, supposes that:

> you have heard of my having arrested Griffiths of Punchcastle [Poyntz Castle] in his own house. The proofs will be brought home to him more than John ... I am credibly informed that the Anabaptists in my neighbourhood above the hills continue to hold nightly meetings since the Fishguard affair, I long to get amongst them but have not been able to quit this town since you left the Country - they have sent me a threatening letter, which I have treated with the contempt it deserved'.[49]

Linked to this assumption is the fact that the French prisoners who gave evidence were paid, but this was within a system of rewards which was common at the time. This point has sometimes been made to show the determination to convict the men, and so make an example of them even though this would have created an injustice. Not only is this payment made explicit in the hearing of the evidence, but it explains a quite bizarre episode in Haverfordwest Castle. It appears that a group of soldiers from the Cardigan Militia, who were on guard, decided to play fives. They found prisoners on the court and ordered them off. They objected, and were therefore put in a dark cell for twenty-four hours. Cawdor happened to visit the castle, and learning of this released the prisoners, and 'before them gave a severe lecture to the sergeant', and told the Frenchmen that the soldiers had acted illegally, and the sergeant 'would be severely punished'. The prisoners asked that the sergeant not be punished, and that they bore no malice. Like prisoners everywhere, they knew better than to upset the gaolers, since, when Cawdor had disappeared, their lives would have been made very unpleasant. Cawdor made the sergeant 'beg their pardon, and gave some money to the prisoners, which set everything to rights'. This is a quite extraordinary happening, since prisoners who had recently been a serious threat, and had now been insubordinate, were indulged in the privilege of hearing an apology from a senior soldier, and were given money. Rutland finishes his narrative with this explanation: 'The reason for this attention to the prisoners was, on account of the evidence which they had in their power to give against the state prisoners, and which, if ill-treated, they might possibly withhold.'[50]

If they were charged only because they were non-conformists, it would seem to have been going to a lot of trouble either to force them to change their faith or to punish them for holding it. It is also possible that in the light of the private conversations between Cawdor and Rutland, this was merely a vindictive prosecution emanating from disgust at the lack of local support.

But there are other possible reasons both for their being charged and for their acquittal. It is possible that they were to be made an example of because of disappointment at the lack of support given by the peasants to the local forces. It is also possible that they *had* colluded with the invaders, and nor would this be surprising in the light of the wretched position of the peasantry, and the considerable discrimination they suffered because of their nonconformity. In this connection, the remarks of Tate to Cawdor should be noted. In his diary, Rutland relates a conversation that Tate had with Cawdor after the surrender. In this Tate said that, 'He had certain information about everything that related to the English forces, that he knew they consisted only of volunteers, and that if his men had remained firm, he might have done all the mischief at first intended.'[51]

The use of the word volunteers is of some interest. It means what it says of course, but in the context of the time it has a specific meaning and an active prosecution would have wondered how Tate came by this information in such a short time. If they had given such information, one is left wondering why it did not encourage Tate to attack. The answer may well be that the speed with which indiscipline helped by the circulation of drink had already, made such action impossible.

A number of other possibilities are suggested by Fenton, writing a few years after the invasion: 'One of them was found within the enemy's lines was proved, and I believe little more; whither, like many others unnoticed, he had been carried by that fool-hardy inquisitiveness, a prominent feature in the character of the low Welsh.' But he adds: 'Not that I shall attempt formally to traverse the indictment, or enter into a vindication of the principles of the accused; poisoned, as by all accounts they probably were, by the seditious publications at that time so industriously disseminated from the corresponding societies in the capital, origo mali'.[52]

It is certainly feasible that people as educated as Griffith could have had access to the seditious material which worried the authorities in Pembrokeshire, as much as anywhere in the country. A specific example which demonstrates that Pembrokeshire, although remote, was not out of touch, may be seen in a letter written on 24 January 1793. Henry Dundas, minister at the Home Office wrote to John Lloyd of Haverfordwest, thanking him for the seditious material mentioned in:

> The Information which you sent to me … I am afraid you will not be able to make out any connection between the pamphlets and Mr. Rees, so as to render him an Offender, but it would be full as desirable if you could bring home the other Charge of seditious Discourses in the pulpit … I have, within these few days heard thro' another Channel of the seditious conduct of Rees, and it would be extremely gratifying, if any Act could be fixed upon him, that would fairly lay him open to Prosecution, perhaps some Plans may be adopted by you, for watching over his proceedings.[53]

Lloyd may have been one of the considerable network of government spies. Since Dundas writes that he had received *two* reports, it seems likely that even Haverfordwest had at least two. As to Rees, he almost certainly was a non-conformist, since no Church of England clergyman at that time would have engaged in 'seditious Discourses in the pulpit'. That the sedition was persistent is shown by a report from Lord Dynevor in March 1795 confirming that seditious material was still circulating in Haverfordwest.[54]

That Samuel Griffith was educated is in no doubt, since Stuart Jones reproduces a letter written by Griffith, in his own handwriting and shown to him by a descendant. Because it is evidence that he was an educated man, and since it represents a rare chance for him to defend himself, it is worth quoting it in its entirety:

> Whereas at a later Great Sessions for the County of Pembroke a most mali-cious prosecution was carried on against me Samuel Griffith a Considerable farmer in the said County, under pretence of High Treason which after several months close confinement [not admitted to Bail] was not permitted to pro-duce my evidence, to confute such false accusation. As also an Unexceptional Character by many Gentlemen assembled for that purpose. But instead thereof exposed to the most Barbarous & malignant bribery and Corruption – Ever exhibited against my life and property to the amount of some Hundreds of pounds, Almost to the entire ruin of myself and Numerous family. By persons who Esteem themselves of rank in the County, who used every Effort, among the Enemies of his Majesty's subjects, who were Impressed for their Liberty – and good usage – and by every Pecuniary method that could be adopted, but on my Trial, it was glossed over as if I had Tampered with the Evidence, being a notorious falsity. Being conscious that my Innocence would protect me. Gentlemen assembled to give me a character were' [The statement stops at this point.][55]

Despite apparently being classified by Fenton as 'low Welsh', Griffith writes here that he is a 'considerable farmer', and Stuart Jones is at pains to point out that his family were notably respectable. One of his broth-ers was an officer in the army and Samuel's eldest son was also a regular army officer, and held several important posts in Pembrokeshire, includ-ing that of Justice of the Peace.[56] However, the respectability of some members of a family does not eliminate the potential or actual delin-quency of others.

The last, in fashionable terms, unspeakable possibility is that they were guilty, at least to some degree. There are several factors which make this at least feasible. The first is the matter of the bay horse with cropped ears. Apologists for the defendants make light of this rather remarkable phenomenon. Stuart Jones is dismissive and scathing about the horse. He writes for example, that in the case of Ashet's evidence, 'it was the horse that mattered to the grenadier'.[57] Jones then deals with some contradictions in the evidence about when John had been seen inside the camp. Dégouy said that while he was with the General: 'one of the French officers rode off on the horse. Apparently he did not get far for the witness said John came out, took his horse and rode away'.[59]

It is possible to argue that, in a world where horses were of paramount importance, the identification of such an exceptional animal would have been critical and had the trial been pursued to the end, much would have been made of this. As to motive, we have already seen that the position of the Pembrokeshire farmer, peasant and worker was so miserable that they could have had little interest in maintaining the existing situation. Nor can the gentry's fear of the poor rebelling be overstated as a factor in the pursuit of these men. As for the collapse of the prosecution because of the French witness's withdrawal, there are a number of possible explanations. Prudhomme, for example, had the highest expectations of being paid, and being sent to America. By the time of the trial there was no sign of that happening.

Or, finally, to put their behaviour in the best possible light, Fenton may have been right when he wrote, in what seem to modern ears patronising terms, following his comment about, 'the low Welsh'. They had, 'a sort of officious temerity, the result of nerve, which if properly directed, would have impelled the possessor to pierce the recesses of the Thuilleries [sic] or St. Cloud, and sheath a poniard in the heart of that disturber of the peace of the world, the execrated Corsican despot.'[59]

However strange, especially non-conformist writers may later have thought of the prosecution of these men, it seemed to come as little surprise to those who were alive at the time. We may wonder now about the motives of the prosecutors, or the truth of the allegations, but it is certain that the accused must have suffered grievously.

The Creation of Myths
and Legends

It should be remembered that these were years of great turbulence. There was still considerable support for the idea of a revolution which would replicate that of the French, nor had the disillusion with what was happening in France properly set in. This would only be consolidated when the Treaty of Amiens broke down in 1803, leading to a resumption of war, and a growing awareness of the real threat posed by Napoleon.

After the invasion therefore, it is not surprising that the authorities saw an excellent opportunity to capitalise on the apparent overthrow of the invading French. This led subsequently to the creation of a persisting version of what had happened, which included brave commanders who had fought against overwhelming odds, and had saved not just the locality, but probably the nation. There is no doubt that in the event they would have done what soldiers have generally done. There were huge and persistent votes of thanks and congratulatory letters. On 4 March 1797, a general meeting of the 'lieutenancy, magistracy &c.', resolved that thanks be given to Knox. The borough of Tenby on 24 March, gave formal thanks to Cawdor, Knox, and others for, 'the zeal, alacrity, and spirited exertions manifested by them, when the French troops effected a landing, near Fishguard, in this county'.[1] A major occasion was the 'General Meeting of the Nobility, Gentlemen, Clergy and Freeholders of the County of Pembroke, and the Town and County of Haverfordwest', convened by Lord Milford, and held in the Guildhall in Haverfordwest on 18 March 1797. At this meeting, thanks were offered to, in order, Cawdor; Colby; Knox; Longcroft; 'all Gentlemen, Yeomen and Peasantry' who served in the several Volunteer corps; the colonel of the New Romney Fencibles; and the officers of that unit, 'for their Ardour and Alacrity, and for the great Expedition with which they marched to the Assistance of this County, and to Lord Milford'. These resolutions were to be printed in the *London Chronicle*, the *Sun*, the *Star*, and Sarah Farley's *Bristol Journal*. We are reminded again of the newspaper contacts which Pembrokeshire had, first drawn to our attention when Philips made his report to Portland about the rioting Hook miners. On that occasion he pointed out that the *Bristol Journal* and other papers found their way to Haverfordwest, and were widely read. The party then repaired to the Castle Inn for a celebration.[2]

An especially fulsome tribute was made to Cawdor probably in April 1797. This took place in St David's Cathedral, and came from 'the Subchanter, and the Vicars Choral'. Here were expressed 'warm- est sentiments of gratitude' and there was reference to 'your Lordship's truly patriotic and noble breast, with which you came as a guardian Angel'.[3] Then there were official letters such as the one of 27 February to Cawdor in which Portland wrote that he was commanded, 'to sig- nify to your Lordship his entire approbation of the judgement zeal and loyalty which has been manifested on the occasion by all orders of his faithful subjects in their respective situations and callings'.[4]

The legends to be examined in this chapter are the reports of massive loyalty and action on the part of local people, the famous story of how the local women in traditional dress deceived the invaders into believ- ing that they were soldiers, and the equally well rehearsed account of the bravery of Jemima Nicholas, who rounded up French soldiers and marched them into captivity.

Examples of bravery and loyalty were reported, exaggerated, and widely disseminated. Reports to London, and many times repeated since, of course, do not take account of the version told to Rutland by Cawdor himself, and set out in Rutland's diary. Much more general is the sentiment expressed in a local contemporary parish entry, from Roch. This refers to: 'The good countenance that the good numbers of peasantry on foot and on horseback w[ith] pikes, pitchforks and scythes exhibited, in the view of the enemy, caused the French officers unani- mously to agree under the Chef de Brigade Tate to propose a surrender … ' The locals are then thanked for 'having gone out against the enemy in the Name of the Lord of Hosts against infidels'. 'Infidels' here refers to Roman Catholics, since it was commonly believed at the time, especially by non-conformists, that the great virtue of the Revolution was that it was attacking and hopefully destroying Popery.[5]

This became established as the standard report of the attitude of the local people, as may be seen in this typical account published in 1875:

> The various roads in the western part of the Principality presented a strange appearance on the Thursday morning, lord and labourer, church member and minister, miner and mechanic, husband and wife, all hastening to bar the enemy's progress by a living wall; and the nearer you got to Fishguard, the more interesting the sight became, for here it was that the brave women of the neighbourhood clad in their red flannel whittles and high felt hats, issued forth from their homes ... and ranging themselves on the adjacent hills, gave the enemy the idea that it was a large body of infantry, preparing to attack them.[6]

We shall review the story of the women later in this chapter.

There was also protest then and later, at perceived demeaning of the behaviour of local people. In March 1797 an Englishman wrote:

> The great attention that seems to be taken by some evil minded people to lessen the merits of the Welch upon the French landing in Pembrokeshire by presenting their numbers as only two or three hundred and absolutely without *any sort of arms* not even *sticks*, requires as it appears to me that the people should be informed of the real state of things and of the gallantry and the loyalty shown by the Welch upon this occasion.[7]

In a rare letter, written by an ordinary citizen at the time, the surrender was described as, 'one of the most glorious conquests ever performed by a parcel of country people.'[8] As far away as Bristol, a newspaper set out an astonishing panegyric:

> When we see how easily the honest Welshmen have repelled the first attempt to make a descent upon our coasts, in a part of the country where, from its nature, there was less military protection than in almost any other, we may conclude how little we have to fear from any attempt the enemy may make in any other quarter. And if we retain, as we are convinced we do, the invincible spirit of Ancient Britons, let the French come whenever they please.

The writer goes on though to remind the readers that:

The inhabitants of that line, extending even nearly as far as North Wales, are chiefly Dissenters and Methodists; and although they have been represented as possessing a strong tinge of democracy, and certainly are not very friendly to the present Administration, they have on this critical occasion shown ample evidence of their aversion to Frenchmen, and attachment to their country. Indeed, we have often been astonished how the enthusiasm and faith which pervade those classes of men could be suspected to be allied to the frequenters of the Parisian Temple of modern Philosophy, or the Courts where death is emblazoned as leading to eternal sleep![9]

While Viscount Hereford wrote that, 'There was never shewn greater spirit & loyalty than in Pembrokeshire. All to a man rose'.[10] Even Stuart Jones, in his magisterial account of the invasion, strongly objects to any suggestion that the local people were in any way deficient in loyalty. He suggests that, 'The general exodus of Wednesday evening was replaced on Thursday morning by a flow of countrymen towards Pencaer, armed with guns, swords, implements of husbandry such as scythes straightened on poles, pitchforks and spades, or anything else they could lay their hands upon.'[11]

Incidentally, this account is clearly drawn, although not acknowledged as such, from the Victorian Harries who is possessed of a vivid imagination, as may be gauged from this account. Following a sermon from a dissenting minister in Carmarthen when, 'he exhorted his audience, for the love of God, to be firm, not to turn their backs to the enemy; assuring them of Divine protection', they all, except the infants and the very old, volunteered 'to go forth with the preacher against the common foe':

This was on Wednesday evening, and by the next morning the whole country was astir, highway and byeway being thronged with national defenders of both sexes, armed with swords and scythes, pistols and pitchforks, guns and reaping hooks, or whatever weapon they could lay their hands upon.[12]

There was indeed no greater advocate of the loyalty of local people than Harries:

In a very short time Haverfordwest heard the news, and was immediately transformed from a quiet country town into an active military centre; while Milford, Pembroke, Tenby, and Narbeth, quivering with excitement, seemed to vie with each other in their exertions to send such a force into the field as would effectually prevent the advance of the enemy. Every gun, pistol, or sword, that could be found, was brought out and made ready for use; while the blacksmiths' shops became suddenly of great importance, for it was there that young and old brought their scythes and reaping-hooks to have them straightened and fixed on poles; and so the quiet blacksmiths were metamorphosed into veritable Tubal Cains, working with might and main, to provide weapons for the volunteers.[13]

Consonant with his wish to applaud the bravery of the local people, H.L.Williams wrote that the French:

Found no conveyance for their ammunition and baggage – no provision, but such as was obtained by plunder, and all the live stock in the neighbourhood were driven into the interior.This is a specimen of Welsh loyalty, though many were accused of being privy to the invasion, and anxious for its success.[14]

We shall go on to see that one of the most accurate, although informal reports on the subject, is that written by the Duke of Rutland. Pointing out that, 'this young nobleman was then but nineteen years of age and had never been in Wales in his life before', Stuart Jones attributes the criticism made of the local people to the fact that they were dissenters. He goes on to suggest that the two Church of England clergymen who accompanied him 'may well have had their share of influence on his opinion'. Rutland was told that, despite there being so many experienced seamen in Fishguard, only one volunteered. But Jones retorts that 'we may be sure that these gallant Welsh seamen would have gladly and cheerfully performed any service which they might have been called for, had matters become really serious'. To which the reply may be fairly made that an invasion by an ostensibly feared enemy just a mile away, was surely serious enough. Jones sums up by saying that 'this kind of thing was jumping to conclusions with a vengeance, and was a gross libel on a most loyal and courageous people'.[15]

Lords Milford and Cawdor told the authorities in London even wilder stories, even though there are contradictions in their accounts. Thus it is claimed that 'the rest of the Forces were Peasants who to some thousands armed themselves with Scythes, Pitchforks &c.'[16] Milford wrote to the Duke of Portland:

The great spirit and loyalty that the Gentlemen and Peasantry have shewn
on this occasion exceeds description, many thousands of the latter having
assembled, armed with pikes scythes, having attacked the Enemy previous to
the arrival of the troops that were sent against them, & many Thousands more
were ready to march could arms have been procured for them.[17]

For demographic reasons alone, this report of 'thousands', is absurd. It
will be remembered that the entire population of Pembrokeshire in the
census of 1801, shortly after this time, was only 56,280. Many of these
were in centres of population at some distance from Fishguard, separated
by rivers, and Milford Haven.

Nor was there agreement about the behaviour of the officers. Milford
wrote to the Duke of Portland on 1 March 1797 in response to a fulsome
expression of thanks from the King and reported that he had passed on
his thanks to the head of each corps. But in a postscript he writes: 'I don't
find that any of the Officers on Half Pay in this county have shewn any
readiness to serve except Ensign Hodges, who has been with us in this
late affair and rendered much assistance'.[18] This is not the official view
expressed by Cawdor in a letter to the Duke of Portland a few days later:
'I have represented to his Royal Highness the Duke of York the merits
of the officers on the half-pay list who contributed to the service.'[19] The
adulation of the people, and most especially of the Yeomanry, is the most
persisting feature of the history of the time, as devised by Victorian commentators. This was even expressed in song, as in the early 1840s when
this ballad was written. This is the first verse and the chorus:

> Now many a day has passed away,
> Since first we marched to Fishguard's shore
> With foreign foes war's game to play
> What Yeomanry ne'er did before;
> Yet on we sped by courage led
> With noble Cawdor took the field.
> Whose skill and spirit at our head
> Invaders soon compelled to yield.
>
> Our rallying word:-
> A good broadsword'
> A nag to bear us fresh and free-

Our ranks enlarge
Then sound the 'Charge'
Bold Castlemartin Yeomanry,
And better men there need not be
Who proudly start from Pembroke's heart,
Her Castlemartin Yeomanry.[20]

Against all of this we have the record afforded by the journal of the Duke of Rutland, who visited the area immediately after the affair was over. His record is based on personal observation; on many conversations with Lord Cawdor who was his host in highly informal circumstances – as the duke points out; and conversations with many people, most of whom had been directly involved in the invasion. Most valuable of all, his diary was not directed at officialdom, nor does it seek to justify or denigrate any action which was taken. Although, as reasonably expected, he is fulsome in his praise of Cawdor.

The first point that must be established is that the situation was a good deal more dangerous than those who describe it as a pantomime would suggest. The duke points out that although such a force could not have done much damage to the country as a whole, 'their numbers were such as to have enabled them to have done more damage than they really did.'[21] This is an echo of an entry made by Wolfe Tone in his diary before the invasion: 'if Tate be a dashing fellow, with military talents, he may play the devil in England before he is caught'.[22] One of the reasons Rutland gives is that although most of the invasion force confirmed to the stereotype of 'dregs' or scum – favourite words in the literature – not all were such:

About six hundred of these men were as fine men, [it may be noted that this was approaching half the force] and as fit for service, as any that ever were employed in any country. The grenadier companies consisted of men all above six feet high, and they were well armed and well equipped.[23]

This is attested to by others as in a document quoted by Salmon: 'the Prisoners are fine looking men – badly cloathed, but well arm'd – Fuselocks new, flints good, and 500 Rounds of ammunition.'[24]

When at Stackpole Court Rutland was shown helmets and swords which had been taken from the French: 'they were all extremely good and serviceable'. These included Tate's own sword 'which was very fine'.[25]

As with so much information and disinformation about the invasion, the
fate of Tate's sword is an example. Kinross says that it is in the hands of
the descendants of Mortimer of Trehowell, and includes a photograph of
it in his book.[26] Perhaps Tate had several. Rutland at one point inspects
French arms in Haverfordwest Town Hall, and notices that the muskets
were 'not so heavy as ours, but were much superior in the springing
of the locks'.[27] The other reasons he gives are of the greatest
significance:

> Had they attacked Lord Cawdor, there was every probability of their being
> successful, and the most serious consequences were to be apprehended from
> the smallness of the English [sic] force, and the little dependence that was to
> be placed upon the country people who had joined them. Those, although
> armed, nevertheless kept themselves aloof, and certainly (had affairs come to
> that crisis) have united themselves with the strongest side, whichever it might
> be.[28]

He goes on however to give 'many instances of particular courage' on
the part of some of the local people.

The duke picked up from his informants a particular distaste for the
people of north Pembrokeshire: 'When I talk of the disaffection of the
peasantry, I must be understood to mean all those around the place where
the enemy landed. They are chiefly Anabaptists … In Carmarthenshire,
and other parts of Wales they would have risen *en masse*'.[29] By this it may
be supposed that unlike Pembrokeshire, in other places they would have
been loyal to the government, but it can be seen that there is a degree of
ambiguity in the sentence.

When he goes to look at the site of the landing, and the scene of subsequent skirmishing, he learns that:

> Fishguard is one of the most disloyal places in Wales. The inhabitants are chiefly
> Anabaptists, and the meeting houses swarm. … During the French invasion,
> only one man turned out as a volunteer from Fishguard, notwithstanding
> between 60 and 80 sail of fishing boats, whose compliment on an average is
> three man, were drawn up on the shore, and their men unemployed.[30]

As to the landing, he points out that:

Certainly they must have had some particular information, [most probably from some of the smuggling or fishing boats] before they could have pitched upon the very spot, where a body of men *might* land. They found themselves as soon as on shore, in an excellent post, defended on two sides by the sea, and on the third by a deep glen, so that they could only be attacked in the front … add to this, the spot where they debarked is totally out of the view of Fishguard, or any of the villages on the coast.[31]

Rutland also draws attention to the fact that the invaders 'expected to be joined by a considerable body of peasantry', since they were carrying such huge quantities of ammunition.[32] This however only tell us of French expectations, not of the conduct of local people. In the course of the day some Frenchmen were standing:

some way from the main body, waving colours, as if to invite the country people to join them. Their standing at a distance from their troops proved that they did not wish to frighten the peasants, and several of the latter rode up and conversed with them during the day.[33]

The cynicism, or fear, of the local gentry – for Rutland was only reporting what he was told – was reflected in another of his visits. This time it was to a house on the outskirts of Haverfordwest which was used as a magazine for the ammunition taken from the French. Here a Mr Nesbitt, who had taken a very active part in the whole business, was in charge of distributing it, 'to arm the loyal inhabitants of the different towns. But great care is used in selecting the fittest men to be entrusted with arms, there being so many disaffected people about the country'.[34] The same anxiety about the control of arms is reflected in a letter from a magistrate, George Bowen of the famous manor of Llwyngwair, which is near Fishguard. It is addressed to Cawdor, and dated 2 March 1797:

In obedience to your Lordship's commands Mr Griffiths and myself have done, and are doing, all in our power for the recovery of such of your prisoners arms and ammunition as were ignorantly carried away by some of the peasants last Friday, who, not thinking it a crime to rob the Enemy, were not a little proud of the trophies, which, however, as soon as required; of them were cheerfully given up to us; but as we didn't find bayonets with the Muskets, it may be prudent to have the prisoners knapsacks searched.[35]

It is, of course perfectly possible that the weapons had been stolen as trophies, as happened amongst the most eminent. A visitor to Stackpole wrote in 1935:

> On various occasions in the past decade, while waiting to start out shooting, I have examined in the front hall of Stackpole Court in Pembrokeshire a curious map and a stand of beautifully polished flint - lock muskets … the stand of arms, thirty nine muskets, formed part of the weapons laid down [after the surrender].[36]

In the case of weapons which came into the possession of the peasantry, it is not fanciful to believe that at least some of these had been handed out in the fulfilment of the original order to encourage the revolt of the local people. It will be recalled that during the treason trials, it was alleged that this had happened.

The reports to Rutland were of unreliability from the peasants. But at least some of the gentry were no better since, 'The gentlemen of the county would never have come forward as they did, had it not been for Lord Cawdor's appointment'.[37] This was a view reiterated by Lord Milford when he wrote in a postscript to the Duke of Portland, as already mentioned: 'I don't find that any of the Officers on Half Pay in this county have shewn any readiness to serve'.[38]

There are also stories about the physical recognition of specific local individuals in the invasion force. These are seemingly definite, but they derive from literature and not from any official or unofficial accounts. As a preliminary to these stories it should be borne in mind that in the search for scapegoats, such people would have been the first to have been targeted, and no doubt put on trial. There is no record of that happening.

There is first the story of James Bowen. In this case John Owen, the master of a sloop, the *Britannia* carrying culm, was boarded by the French in the bay, and he was taken on board the *Vengeance* for questioning. Harries and others write that the French, having taken anything useful, sank her.[39] On the ship he recognised a man, and Jones believes, quoting H.L. Williams, 'there are grounds for thinking that this man was one James Bowen'. He had been a farm servant at Trehowel, but had been dismissed and transported for horse stealing. Somehow, it has been supposed, he escaped or he was captured and ended up in France.

From there, again it is supposed, he volunteered to sail with the French in order to escape, 'and possibly getting his own back on his former master'.[40] If this were judged to be true, it would have to be accepted that a prisoner of war would have known what the expedition was about, even though Hoche had been extremely careful to keep the business secret, so secret in fact that even British Intelligence knew nothing of it, and that after the event, one of the prisoners was so ignorant that he asked if they were in Ireland. This leaves aside the fact that the landing in Pembrokeshire was not the original intention. It is further suggested that he may have guided the French to their anchorage, and that he suggested Trehowel as a headquarters.[41] H.L. Williams, in his version, notes that when Mortimer returned to Trehowel, his servant Ann George saw a man and her 'Suspicions were aroused by his manner, to which her attention had been drawn by a neighbouring female, advanced towards, and instantly recognised him, and said "James Bowen, what are you doing here?" to which he made no reply'.[42]

It should be remembered though that Trehowel *is* near, arguably the nearest, substantial building to the landing point. This raises the question once again as to the reliability of H.L. Williams, since he goes on to say that the 'commodore' ... 'bade him [Owen, the captain] sleep behind his back', and in the morning gave him permission 'to go and see his wife and children, under a promise of returning in three hours:- he went but did not return.'[43]

With regard to this specific case of James Bowen, it can be argued that in his evidence after the surrender, St Leger (who had been sent to establish a headquarters at Trehowel), makes no mention of Bowen whose idea it allegedly was. Rose also produced very firm evidence when he wrote: 'I have searched through the Great Sessions and Quarter Sessions papers from 1790 up to 1797 and there simply was no James Bowen transported for horse stealing or any other crime'.[44]

One person Stuart Jones heard about from a personal source was a former *gwas mawr* (head servant) of Llanwnwr, identified by David Cornock - a blacksmith from Newbridge near Letterston, when the soldiers rested there. Jones' theory is that he had been a prisoner of war, and 'had offered his services as an interpreter in the hope of escape'.[45]

Another Victorian writer, Laws, recounts how a respectable man named Meyler, overheard two of the prisoners speaking Welsh:

'Where do you come from', said he, 'as you speak Welsh?'

'We come from the upper part of Pembrokeshire'.

'Then how come you to be soldiers in the French army?'

'We have been taken prisoners in the French army, and were taken out with the other convicts'.

'Then why don't you leave them?'

'Because we are afraid of being discovered and shot'.

They then asked Meyler to apprise their friends of their whereabouts.[46] Laws has in fact taken this story, changing a few insignificant details, from H.L. Williams.[47] But Laws also lays personal claim to a version which he reports:

> Mr. Bowen of Fynondrudion informed the writer that his grandfather fled from Fynondrudion with his family and servants to Wolf's Castle. After the capture of the French they went out on the roadside to see the prisoners go by. One of the maidservants recognised an aquaintance in the ranks, and the man called out 'ie a thyna Catrin Trerhonw hefyd', Englished [sic] 'And there is Catrin of Trerhonw, too'.[48]

This however looks very like a version by H.L. Williams in which he reports a prisoner addressing 'a woman by her name, and also mentioned her residence in the Welsh language'.[49]

Can such stories of particular individuals being identified be true? What gives them some credibility is that it is quite possible that they had been prisoners of war and had been forced, or volunteered, to join the expedition, although their motives or the mechanism by which they did so are not clear. The other factor adding to their credibility is that their personal details are so specific, and that the individuals who recognised them are also clearly identified. Doubt arises however on a number of counts. The first of these is that it would have to be accepted that there were so many prisoners of war in France from such a thinly populated area as Pembrokeshire. Furthermore, the authorities were not unwilling to prosecute local people for treason. It might be supposed that since they had borne arms against their country they would have been prime candidates for prosecution, especially since it would have become clear who they were during the long period of imprisonment they were about to undergo. Portland was quite specific about this when he wrote:

'Not to omit it on any account should Gen. Wall, or any other subject of his Majesty who appears to have any command, be found among the prisoners.'[50]

One of the most enduring legends of the invasion is that of the parading of Welsh women in their traditional dress, and the invaders believing them to be soldiers. The sources of this story are very tortuous.

It was alleged at the trial of Thomas John that he reported that (speaking of the British force), 'there were only three hundred below'. This figure was challenged by the French, who said it looked like there were more. John replied that 'half were women with red flannels'. The often stated belief is that these French witnesses, or strictly in this case an American, Charles Prudhomme, was being paid to lie so that the defendants would be convicted. It seems an odd detail for such a witness to invent, and actually tends to give strength to the allegation against John that he was in the French camp discussing the disposition of the British. It also gives some mild support to the claimed visibility of the Welsh women, but stops short of the legend, neither is this slight connection usually marshalled as evidence.

The first piece of evidence commonly advanced to support the claim of the activity of the women concerns two prints. The first of these is a caricature entitled *A Fishguard Fencible*, and the second *A Welch Peasant and his wife*. The first depicts a substantial figure wielding a bill hook, with a leek in his hat and the motto *ich dien* attached to it. A caption reads: 'Py St. David's - They took the Womens Cloaks for Soldiers & look'd as pale as the Tiffel himself'. The second, entitled 'A Welch Peasant and his Wife', shows a man holding a sickle, and a woman a pitchfork:

> In their accustomed Habits, and with the kind of Weapons that several Thousand People appeared with near Fishguard Feby 24th 1797 the Day the French surrendered to Ld. Cawdor & Colonel Colbey's [sic] Troops. The wonderful Effect that the Scarlet Flannel had that Day should never be forgotten … Lord Cawdor very Judiciously placed a considerable number of Women in that Dress, in the rear of his Army, who being considered by the French as regular Troops, contributed in no small degree to that happy and unexpected Surrender.

Unfortunately, these prints display weaknesses when considered as evidence. The first is that although Jones writes of the Fencible that it is 'of

date March 1797', this is not clear. It should be added that the caption
could not have been written by a Welshman, since it is in the language
of Shakespeare or the music hall. With regard to the second, there is no
date, or evidence of date on this print, which eliminates any evidential
value which might be put upon it. We might note in passing, that here
again Knox, who provided the biggest contingent and whose 'Fencible'
is the subject, is not mentioned. If these prints were really produced so
quickly, it would have been before his 'disgrace'.

Two contemporary letters are sometimes used to support the myth of
the women, both written on the same day in February 1797. The first is
from John and Mary Mathias of Narbeth to their sister in Swansea. In it
they tell her of the invasion, and how people from all parts of the county
went to see what was happening. Included were 'near four hundard
Women in Red flanes', and 'they thought the women to Be a Ridgment
of Soldiers'.[51] The second letter was from John Mends of Haverfordwest
to his son in Essex. In this he writes that there were 'about 400 poor
women with Red flanel over their Shoulders, which the French at a
distance took for soldiers, as they appeared all Red'.[52] These are noteworthy because they are so close to time and place. But placed against all
the other evidence, or rather lack of it, they cannot be true. It is possible
that the story was already beginning to circulate, although it was to be a
long time before it surfaced again. It should be noted too that Mends is
not accurate in other statements he makes. For example, he writes that
'because of the vigilance, alacrity, and spirit of the Welch … in about 48
hours they amounted to about 7 or 8 Thousand men of all sorts', a figure
which, as has already been pointed out was demographically impossible.

H.L.Williams also refers to the matter, although, surprisingly his claims
are less definite or dramatic than some: 'It was a grand spectacle, to look
on the surrounding hills, crowded with innumerable spectators of both
sexes: – the women in their scarlet mantles and round hats, appeared at a
distance like so many soldiers.'[53]

Rose discovered two letters of interest, which had been deposited in
the National Library of Wales as recently as 1973. The first of these, dated
25 February 1797, was written by a Quaker, Ann Knight, who seems to
have been visiting Haverfordwest. This is of prime interest because it is
an eye witness account of the arrival of the French prisoners, and the
fear that their arrival engendered. But she too refers to the women: 'the
English or rather Welsh got together all the women and children with

the red flannels over their shoulders and placed them in such a position that the french could only see their heads and they thought it was a large army of men'.[54] This is supposed to have occurred *before* the surrender, and although Rose is pleased to have unearthed this letter, he does urge caution. He points out that the remarks about the women are hearsay, and that some statements in the letter are very questionable, such as that which suggests that the French prisoners already incarcerated in Pembroke had killed five of the newly arrived invaders because they had surrendered. And although having said that Ann Knight was referring to the surrender, Rose concludes 'that the traditional story is substantially true'.[55] It must be made clear though that the evidence is confined to a presence of women, naturally wearing traditional dress *at some time*, which is far removed from being armed, or being paraded. With regard to the killing of French prisoners, H.L. Williams writes that 'many died on board, being confined under deck'. He then lists three killed, presumably meaning in skirmishes, three wounded, and two died, but offers no proof of 'the many' who died on board.[56]

The grandson of the well known historian Fenton added considerable weight to the legend, because of his family name. He 'was assured by his father, uncle, and old Fishguardians', that 'Campbell' (Cawdor):

> Ordered all the women of the countryside and places to be wrapped in the long red cloaks then universally worn by Welshwomen, and supplying as many as he could with real muskets and bayonets, and others with stakes, pokers, and the old fashioned roasting spits, lined the stone walls from the Bryn-y-Mor to Manorowen, with those brave lasses in their tall steeple-crowned hats, to make the French (whom he knew would advance across Goodwick Sands in the hope that some stores would be landed there) believe they were in the face of overwhelming force.[57]

It is inconceivable that Cawdor would have handed out arms to women even supposing they knew how to use them, when allegedly there were men who were carrying only farm tools. It may also be asked how 'Campbell' would have known of an advance across Goodwick Sands.

David Davies, in an otherwise serious and respected book, seems to falter in his scholarship as many have done, when faced with the massive mythology of the invasion. He writes offering a slightly different version, the reliability of which may be judged in the light of other errors in his narrative of the invasion. In it he writes that, 'Captain Harries, a veteran who had been fighting in the war with America, took command of the Yeomanry of Castle Martin, the Cardiganshire Militia, and the Cardiff Militia, who chanced to be in Pembrokeshire, at the time'. These statements are manifestly totally wrong, since there is no record of a Captain Harris being present, or in the army list of the regiments who were there. Nor was there present 'the Cardiff Militia', another inaccuracy which has been enshrined and passed on.[58] So when he goes on to make his contribution to the women in red shawls, his accuracy has to be questioned: 'As a diversion, he also (it is persistently asserted by local tradition), urged the women to wear their red shawls and tall hats, and march within sight of the enemy'.[59] Stuart Jones adduces some support from Sir John Fortescue, 'meticulous historian of the British army', who wrote that the French were overawed: 'By detachments of the Cardigan Militia and of other local levies, and by the red cloaks of the Welsh women who crowned the surrounding hills to witness so interesting a spectacle'.[60] However, Fortescue was published in 1906 by which time the legend would have been widely known. It was even well known in France. In *The Times* of Tuesday 17 December 1859 there appears a letter from Edouard Tate, surely a relation of the French commander, since he writes in a criticism of a Mr Ridgway that the version of events he claims, 'Is not founded upon any French authority, nor is it founded on the exaggerated recollections or predilections of any of my own family: it is wholly founded on the official English account of the transaction'.

It is also clear that although seemingly writing from Leicester Square, he lives in France, since he goes on: 'Lord Cawdor, (whom I erroneously styled "Count", a title I am informed you have not in England)'. He then mentions the women in red: 'Mr. Ridgway further discloses that it was M. Tate's messenger bearing the letter offering to surrender and not M. Tate himself, who is supposed to have been imposed upon by the red petticoats of the Welshes [sic] and the various uniforms of the volunteers'.

Stuart Jones, with characteristic thoroughness, also draws attention to a work by Captain Desbrière published in 1902. In this, Desbrière repeats the familiar story, this time to 'pour scorn upon the expedition'. But as Jones goes on to point out he is 'apparently quoting from the work of Miss ME James, (1897) in itself a mixture of history and fiction'.[61] And the ever fanciful H.L. Williams relates how:

A French lady of rank who was making a tour through England and Wales, visited the camp at Pencaer, - said, when at home, she had often heard, that her countrymen had been frightened by the Welsh women's mantles, mistaking them for British soldiers. She purchased one of the scarlet flannels, to take home to France, in order to ridicule the French military.[62]

The legend has even become locked into French history: 'Our countrymen, seeing figures on the cliffs wearing red tunics surrendered to the British soldiers without a struggle to the Welsh in their local costume'.[63]

The story has had, as it still does, enormous appeal. The truth is probably that there may well have been women about in the traditional red cloaks, though how many it is impossible to guess. There could not possibly have been the 400 alleged in the letters. Several of those who document the events point out that, beginning with Mrs Harries of Tregwynt, women had very wisely rushed away from the scene as quickly as they could. Jones points out that 'most of the women folk had got away on the previous evening'.[64] It is possible that Cawdor asked in passing, and as a joke, if they would want to fight, although there is no record of this, and yet somehow this became enshrined. It is also possible that when local people assembled, apparently in large numbers to see the surrender, there would have been substantial numbers of women in traditional dress, and somehow the presence of these on the skyline was somehow transmuted into their having been there before the surrender.

But what really must reduce this excellent story to rubble is that, considering what an extraordinary action it would have been, there is no mention of it in any of the many official reports and communiqués, nor most significant of all does Cawdor refer to it; even in the long and frank accounts he gave to the Duke of Rutland. The nearest Rutland comes to mentioning anything which could be construed as supporting the story is when he writes: 'The peasants who had assembled were so artfully arranged, as to appear to the French as if the whole country had risen *en masse*'.[65] But he is, in any case, writing about the surrender and not specifically about women, although no doubt some would have been there.

Salmon, who was a very well informed commentator and extremely well acquainted with all possible documentation, dismisses Fenton and the legend abruptly: 'not one word of this is true'.[66] The Reverend Vincent, who it will be remembered was born in Fishguard in 1799, 'was also sceptical about "the story often repeated and sometimes believed that the French had been induced to submit so speedily in consequence of their having mistaken the red flannels of the women for soldiers'".[67]

But the legend cannot easily be put down. In 1875 John Harries wrote a book about the invasion which was dedicated:

> To: the women of Pembrokeshire
> Descendants of the brave whittle weavers
> Who struck terror
> Into the hearts of the
> Invaders
> This Little Book
> Is most respectfully dedicated.

And as recently as 1980, a German archivist wrote to the Pembrokeshire record office: 'As I understand the women of Fishguard are told to have beaten off the French invaders in 1797 ... I should appreciate any information about those brave women of Fishguard'.[68]

Lloyd George's great-grandfather farmed Tresinen or Tresinwen, about a mile from the invasion site, and this farm is listed by H.L. Williams as one of the houses looted. Lloyd George, never one to miss a chance to indulge in hyperbole, went so far as to claim that his great grandmother had organised the women![69]

It is arguable that this role of opposition to the 'enemy' which is allocated to women, is of much greater significance than a rather jolly piece of local folklore. More generally, it has long been recognised that women have wielded enormous influence on public affairs. Bruce, in her book on Napoleon and Josephine, reminds us that:

> It was the women ... who set the tone of the intellectual and political life of the capital [Paris]. In this deeply feminized society their authority had been rooted for over a century in the tradition of the salons. Never in French history, however, had their power been greater than it was then as arbiters of ethics and politics and in molding public opinion.[70]

It is, however, time to recognise that it was not only aristocratic women who have been made an insistent force for change. Humbler women from the peasants of France to the miners' wives of Hook have made an impact on the direction of political and social events. The truth about the behaviour of women in British, especially Welsh, history when there has been social turbulence, is that they have been in the forefront of the protests. This was the case in Northampton in 1693 where 'great numbers of them [came] into the market place with knives stuck in their girdles',[71] and in Essex in 1709, 'mobs of women amounting to hundreds were on the move, threatening to burn houses, and shoot corn dealers'.[72]

In Wales, that contribution has been described as a 'history of omission'.[73] And even if protest did not lead to dramatic change, it was a persistent and, for the authorities, threatening problem. Thus in Haverfordwest in 1644, 'the poorest sort of women' attacked officials who were trying to collect taxes.[74] Women were out in force in Swansea in 1793 where 'they were amongst the most vocal and extreme members of the mobs'.[75] In Cardiganshire, during protests over enclosures in 1815: 'A mob comprised solely of women, and armed with dripping pans, came down upon John Hughes and his helpers "like a rolling torrent" ... they directed his attention to a pit which had been dug for the internment of every surveyor who approached their "rights"'.[76]

In the specific case of the French Revolution, it is a commonplace that women took a commanding, critical, and continuing part as events unfolded. They were, for example, determined to make Louis XVI's return to Paris from Versailles and provided the physical force to make him do so. This has been expressed in rather nationalistic terms, but the summary is no less accurate for that:

> Such things are not only seen in France; our women are brave, and make others so. The country of Joan of Arc, Joan of Montfort, and Joan Hachette can cite a hundred heroines. There was one at the Bastille, who afterwards departed for war, and was made captain in the artillery; her husband was a soldier. On the 18th of July, when the king went to Paris, many of the women were armed. The women were in the van of our Revolution. We must not be surprised; they suffered more.[77]

On this occasion in Versailles, Lecointre, the Lieutenant Colonel 'addressed himself to the regiment of Flanders, and asked the officers and soldiers whether they would fire. The latter were already under a far more powerful influence. Women had cast themselves among them entreating not to hurt the people'.[78]

Any government would recognise that such a spirit is extremely dangerous, and has to be reigned in. Their problem is that there is no doubt that when there is deprivation, it is the women and their children (for it is assumed that the children are *their* responsibility), who suffer the most. The task for the government, and this was the case in Britain in the 1790s and after, is to somehow persuade women that although times may be hard, they would be a good deal worse if there were any breakdown in the social order, not to say a full-scale revolution.

At the time of the French threat of invasion, and especially after Fishguard showed that it was at least feasible, several writers dwelt specifically on the fate of women if it happened again. In a typical piece, an exhortation to the people of Britain, and the Chirk volunteers, 'and all Welshmen in particular', a man called Holland Price wrote:

> The shrieking virgin from the spoiler flies
> And fills the valleys with her piercing cries,
> He heeds them not, but seizes on his prey,
> And bears in triumph the poor maid away[79]

This is the context within which this fabrication about the red cloaks was nurtured, and also helps to explain the emphasis commonly given to the shouting at prisoners which is recounted by Cawdor writing to his wife: 'And thro' Wales, tho' the indignation of the people was great, I found my influence would protect them without difficulty. The women were more clamorous than the men, making signs to cut their throats, and desiring that I would not take the trouble of carrying them further'.[80] And we have seen that during the food riot in Haverfordwest by Hook miners in 1795, their women took an active part.

Within the persisting myth, is one that is even more reluctant to be shed. It is that amongst all the brave women there was one who was physically notable. At the time, there was no investment in the myth of the 'gallant Welsh women', or the remarkable 'Amazon' Jemima. This was Jemima Nicholas of Fishguard. So entrenched is the Jemima myth that she features prominently in the tapestry woven to commemorate the invasion, and has a commemorative stone in the churchyard of St Mary's, Fishguard. Quinault[81] points out that the first reference to this story is in the publication by H.L. Williams in 1842, and this quotation by the latter sums up the essence of the story:

Jemima Nicholas, an inhabitant of the town of Fishguard, a tall stout, masculine female, who worked as a shoemaker and cobbler, felt imbued with the noble and patriotic spirit of Ancient Cambria - she took a pitchfork and boldly marched to Pencaer ... on her approach she saw, in a field, about twelve Frenchmen, not a whit daunted she advanced to them and whether alarmed at her courage, or persuaded by her rhetoric, she had the address to conduct them to, and confine them in the guardhouse, in Fishguard church.[82]

This is yet another example of the common acceptance of William's stories. Kinross, for instance, reports this as a matter of fact.[83] David Davies adds another dimension. He writes that: 'One woman, named Jemima Nicholas, took into the British camp six Frenchmen, under the pretence that they, having lost their way, were being taken by her to the French Camp'.[84] It may be noted that the number of prisoners she took varies from version to version. When she died in 1832, the vicar of Fishguard wrote in the parish register: 'The woman was called Jemima Vawr ie. Jemima the Great, from her heroine acts, she having marched against the French who landed hereabouts in 1797, and being of such personal powers as to be able to overcome most men in a fight. I recollect her well'.[85]

Her memorial stone records her as 'The Welsh Heroine who boldly marched out to meet the French invaders'. Once again there is no contemporary report of such a remarkable feat. What is consonant with the spirit of Pembrokeshire is the belief of Rev. Henry Vincent, a local vicar who knew her and 'whom he remembered clearly'. Her feat was, he felt, enhanced by the amount of drink she was given.[86] Rose also rightly points out that she was not given a pension which might have been expected, although a measure of the growth of legend can be gauged from the fact that some writers state that she did;[87] he mentions Carradice[88] as one who perpetuates the myth.

The tales raise a general problem about the reliability of oral history, especially if there is no documentary version to support it. Syd Walters, a local man from Goodwick, is a classic example as his account is based, as he would claim, on oral tradition handed down in his family. The weaknesses of that tradition are compounded by a loathing of Roman Catholics, and a detestation of the Pembrokeshire squires, especially in the south of the county which, as we have seen, led him to write of collusion between Mortimer of Trehowel, Knox, and the French officer Barry St Leger. One may doubt the truth of stories which have been passed down by word of mouth, but occasionally some, however unlikely, can be corroborated. Such a story concerns an incident in the farmhouse of Brestgarn, at the time occupied by Rev. David Bowen. It is related how a drunken French soldier, assuming that the ticking of the grandfather clock was a human noise, shot at it. The verification lies in the fact that the clock, with the bullet hole clearly visible, is still in Brestgarn.

So we have in the history of the invasion a challenge to the reliability of oral evidence, since in the final analysis most of the evidence is oral, hearsay or second-hand. This book is replete with questions on the subject, and we have noted many examples of this. In summary, one will suffice. Thus H.L. Williams parades the facts as presented by people who were there at the time, as beyond dispute. And at the time he was writing he could have been honest in that, or at least he could have been forgiven for believing them. But apart from the validity of his informants, there is the question of the lack of attention to detail of Williams himself. The utterly vital nature of this, as has been shown, lies in the way in which versions of events have been perpetuated, because they appeal. This was a strange and remarkable event, and local people suddenly becoming the focus of national events could hardly be blamed for indulging in the fame of it all —especially since the powerful in the district encouraged the enjoyment of victory over the 'enemy'. We can be reminded of the local nineteenth-century clergyman, not unduly cynical, who implicitly urged caution about local accounts when he wrote: 'the natives had the opportunity of refreshing their memories, fighting their battles over again and spinning long yarns which they turned to a more speedy and in a pecuniary point of view, to a more profitable account than the webb [sic] of Penelope'.[89]

The truth, and in some ways the pity of it, is that the invasion has been embroidered beyond credibility, and that the principal myths upon which the story rests are at best questionable. This is in no way to diminish the dignity of the people of Pembrokeshire in 1797, who struggled against and survived every adversity. For them alone, in the light of their struggles, this may not have been a 'pantomime', even though it may have been a sideshow in the war against France. For the people of Pembrokeshire, this was a dangerous matter.

Epilogue

The first problem the British faced, after the invasion, was the disposal of the French prisoners. There were already many French prisoners in Britain. The British government did not want to keep them indefinitely, as Portland made clear to Milford in a letter of February 1797:

> It will be the first object of Government to relieve the Country from the burthen and anger of keeping these wretches and I have the honor to inform your Lordship *in confidence* that measures are actually in contemplation for sending them back to France.
>
>   Your Lordship will however be so good as not to mention this intention to anybody but Lord Cawdor, but endeavour to make such an arrangement respecting the places of their confinement as may be most suitable for their speedy embarkation.[1]

After all the movements on the part of various groups of prisoners, the bulk of those who had survived were exchanged for the prisoners of the French. Some were royalist sympathisers and they naturally had no wish to return to France. There was friction between these and the main, republican body of prisoners, and some of the royalists were recruited into the British army. Within eighteen months most of the officers had been released, including Tate, who was discharged on parole on 24 November 1798. The Irish officers were the subject of a discussion as to whether they could be charged with treason. In a report to the duke of Portland, the view of the Crown law officers (the Attorney-General and the Solicitor-General), was that there were grounds for prosecution. They were, after all, technically British subjects.[2] But the decision was difficult because of the presence of royalist prisoners who had fought for the British, presently being held in French prisons. Reprisals in such a case seemed a distinct possibility, and on that account they were not charged. They were lucky that they were not as eminent as Wolfe Tone.

Tate returned to Paris, and Stuart Jones, drawing upon valuable French sources went to some lengths to trace his career afterwards. Tate seems to have begun to rehabilitate himself by trying to recover recognition of his rank as *Chef de Brigade*, and even appealed directly to Barras, the president of the directory, making the point that he had carried out his orders to invade, but had faced a superior force. Eventually he was awarded half pay. But he was not employed on military service again. In 1809, the police opened a file on him. This was because of debts amounting to some £8,000 to £10,000, accumulated in part, Stuart Jones suggests, because 'he had been living with a lady friend of extravagant habits and of the name of Genselle'. The debts were eventually settled somehow but before that, in April of the same year, the American ambassador in Paris wrote to Tate and told him of a ship in Dunkirk bound for America. There followed somewhat protracted negotiations with the Minister of War, Tate beginning these by stating his expectation that America and Britain might go to war, and he could take part on the American side. Eventually, and after the police had been consulted, he was given permission to leave. This was the last that was heard of him.[3]

One of the effects of the invasion was a realisation that an attack could happen anywhere. Because of the alarm caused by the invasion of Pembrokeshire, albeit short lived, many parts of the country were nervous in case of another attack, naturally with Pembrokeshire being especially apprehensive. In a letter to Portland, Milford reflects this new concern that better precautions should be taken: 'As every thing is now quiet I intend taking a survey tomorrow of the Sea Coast & to pitch upon proper places for Beacons'.[4] It seems that the view that any attack would be made in the east of England had been modified: 'It is the opinion of men of the first military talents, that in case the French were ever to invade Great Britain, they would commence by a descent on the coast of Cardigan or Pembroke'.[5]

As quickly as 28 February 1797 the first alarm was raised. Although H.L. Williams does not enter a date, he is the source of the following detail. A Mr John Roach, seemingly being anxious about another attack was watching the coast near St David's. It was dark, and he heard several boats approaching the shore and dropping anchor. Certain that it was another invasion he sent a message to St David's, and the cathedral organist rode the sixteen miles to Haverfordwest in forty-five minutes. After receiving his report, the mayor called a meeting, drums beat to arms 'and the necessity of putting all the French prisoners to death, solemnly debated'.[6] It then became clear that this was a false alarm. The vessels were apparently coasters bound for Milford, who had anchored and were waiting for the tide. They had sent in their boats to rob the fishing nets. Cawdor made an entry in his diary: 'Alarms of landing near St. David's & in Gower. Town in confusion the whole night. Gen. Rooke arrived at 7 o'clock pm'.

Rooke, now in charge in Pembrokeshire, wrote at once to the Lord Lieutenant of Carmarthenshire that he should ensure the security of the French prisoners in Carmarthen, 'as a report is previously here that the enemy is landing'.[7] The result was that the prisoners were locked up in Carmarthen Castle, and the town was thrown into pandemonium, with townspeople mustering arms, and the quick despatch of the Light Romney Fencible Dragoons to Pembrokeshire.

According to Stuart Jones, the Gower rumour originated with a message from Thomas Mansel Talbot to the Portreeve of Swansea that there had been a landing in Rhossilly Bay. Some of the Swansea volunteers went to investigate, but found nothing.[8] This rumour was sent in a message from the mayor of Kidwelly to Carmarthen, which exacerbated the confusion.[9] The reports of these two landings had reached the admiralty and as a consequence, orders were sent to Sir Edward Pellew, then at Plymouth, to sail up the Bristol Channel. Now a fresh rumour emanated from a Captain Gibbes, the regulating officer in Swansea. This was that there was a landing at Newquay on the coast of Cardiganshire. Pellew was now instructed to take on board arms and ammunition, which was to be handed out to servicemen, and to local people. Pellew set sail with a small squadron of ships, and was soon off the coast of Pembrokeshire. Paradoxically this set off another alarm, since the local people thought they were French. H.L. Williams, engaging in his familiar mixture of hyperbole and ultra loyalty describes what happened:

It would be impossible to describe the scene of confusion and dismay which took place: women in tears, and fainting; – the men crying, 'to arms! to arms!'. Every church and chapel, from St. David's to Fishguard, sent forth its quota of brave defenders; and many hundreds of bold and determined hearts had assembled in Fishguard, resolved to conquer or die.[10]

After an exchange of news, Pellew now sailed up the coast to try to discover what was happening at Newquay. Here they discovered that there had been no landing, nor threat of a landing, as Pellew made clear in a dispatch to the admiralty on 8 March.[11]

The next rumour of invasion came about a month later, when Colby wrote the following letter to the mayor and magistrates of Carmarthen. It is undated, but the letter which he encloses is marked as 6 April 1797 at 10.30 p.m. from Haverfordwest:

> On the other Side is a Copy of a letter which I have this instant forwarded to Lord Cawdor & the troops in the neighbourhood - as it is apprehended a landing may be effected in the course of the night I think it is my Duty to apprize the Country in general with those Circumstances be so good as to forward a copy of this letter by the Mail tomorrow to Lt. Gen. Rooke as Military Duty will require my presence immediately.

The letter:

> To Cawdor
> My Lord,
> Mr. Nesbitt Mr. D Bowen 7 & a Sailor observed *three* [his italics] large three Mast Ships some Cutters and Briggs, in the whole 13 Sail off Garnfawr near Fishguard at an early hour in the morning, two trading Sloops on approaching them were seen to tack round & croud all sail & run away. Mr. Nesbitt [word torn off margin ? sent] this Information *express* about three o'clock.
>
> Mr. Dd. Bowen & the Sailors continued observing them, they lay too off the Bishop & Clerks till late in the evening when they sailed seemingly as if standing round for Milford, they were observed forming a Line several times during their laying too - prior to their Sailing late in the evening part of them were observed to take two Sloops, this information Mr. Noot brought from Fishguard at the request of Mr. Dr. Bowen - he left Fishguard a little after six o'clock this evening-during the time of their laying too off the Bishop and Clerks two of their Cutters ran several time close in shore-it has been very hazy the whole of the day at Sea there - Capt. Longcroft who is now with me supposes that it is not likely that the Inhabitants about St. David's could

discover them – Capt. Longcroft sent out his little Cutter at 5 o'clock this
evening to observe their motions with orders that if they were enemies to
go for Cork & give Information and has also sent to Capt. Dobbins about
nine o'clock to go out and watch them – Orders were also sent for his men
to repair to their guns opposite the Stack Rock – I have sent this open with
Orders for the Messenger to shew it to Major Ackland as he passes his house –
your Lordship will of course forward it to Capt. Ackland and the other Corps
on your side the water –
I am in haste
Your Lordship's faithful friend
J Colby[12]

There was no doubt that on this occasion, which *The Times* reported on
15 April 1797, the ships which had been seen were a fleet of merchantmen. But it may be supposed that after the actual invasion experience,
Colby's seemingly frenetic activity was excusable. It is difficult to recap-
ture the primitive nature of communications in that period, and the
inevitable ignorance which people had to endure as to what was happening in nearby districts, not to say in other parts of the country.

There were other repercussions which were much more serious than
false rumours of invasion. Probably the most important of these was the
effect on the Bank of England. The Bank was going through a difficult
time at the end of the eighteenth century. The difficulties were compounded at the beginning of 1797 because of the fear of invasion. Pitt
was relaxed about major attacks, 'but would not "answer that no partial
attack would be made"'. The invasion in Pembrokeshire was the 'partial
attack'. This led 'to so much excitement or confusion', and when the
King and the leaders had a meeting on 26 February, this led eventually
to the 'era of suspension which was to last so very much longer than the
Bank or the ministers can have imagined'.[13] This indeed was one of the
objects of an invasion, and the French government was well aware of
the vulnerability of the Bank: 'In the House of Commons Dundas had
proclaimed that the destruction of private and public credit had been
the enemy's prime motive in the expeditions to Ireland and Wales, and
the only object they could have hoped to achieve'.[14]

The fear of another invasion remained, until the demonstration of
British sea supremacy was established beyond question. There was an
especial flurry of activity after the breakdown of the Treaty of Amiens in

1803 and the resumption of war, when it appeared that Napoleon was preparing for an invasion, evidenced by his amassing of ships and troops in western France. At a meeting in the Castle Inn in Haverfordwest on 24 of October 1803, addressed by Major General Gascoyne, it was recognised that Pembrokeshire was as vulnerable as any part of the country and so:

> It is strongly to be recommended that no further time be lost in calling forth the energy of the county of Pembroke; the General commanding the District cannot but remark that this country which from its local situation, as well as from the peculiar circumstances of a Landing having been effected during the last War, by a very small Body of Troops: also from its contiguity to Ireland, which part of the Kingdom offers the greatest encouragement and temptation to the *French* to invade.

Yet it was admitted in the course of the preparations that:

> The General commanding the District, takes leave to inform the County, that Government is not sufficiently acquainted with the actual defenceless state of these coasts; and it cannot for a moment be doubted that they imagine this District is in danger, and the County of Pembroke in particular, when it is considered that this is the only County from hence to the Metropolis wherein the Volunteers are called into permanent Pay and Duty.

The Major General's hope was that: 'However painful may be the reflection to him on the present defenceless state of this County, he has a reliance [that when he seriously informs them the County is threatened with the immediate danger of attack] that their future exertions will make up for lost time'.[15]

In a series of meetings it was announced that there were to be three dimensions to the preparations. The first was to be a series of warnings if a landing seemed imminent, or took place, and so a series of signal and fire beacon posts should be set up. Secondly, that there should be an inventory of livestock, carts, and carriages. Elaborate arrangements were then put in place to ensure their removal from the coast, no doubt in part to ensure their survival and in part to ensure that they were beyond the reach of the invaders. Thirdly, there should be mobilisation of men. The Yeomanry Cavalry should be stationed so that they could communicate with Cardiff, and a body of volunteer pioneers should be established, 'whose advanced period of life might better suit with this employment than that of Arms. They should be furnished with Pick-axes, Spades, and each a Sword if to be procured'.[16] One of the last links with the invasion was the resolution that 'Mr Charles Hassall be appointed Major of Pioneers in the County of Pembroke, and Captains of Hundreds are requested to make all returns to him'. Hassall, it seems, was still believed to be reliable and skilled by the authorities.[17]

General Rooke took an especial interest in Tenby, and Captain Ackland was sent in early March to assess the state of the defences of the town:

> When he desired that the Gentlemen of the Corporation would remove or cause to be removed Two Guns Eighteen Pounds on each, now lying on the pier in the said Borough and placed upon the Castle where the same are to remain until further Orders from the said General. And Whereas it is ordered this ninth day of March One thousand seven hundred and ninety seven, that Capt. John Griffiths of the said Borough be appointed to take charge of Procuring Hands to convey the said Guns To the Castle [the place appointed] as aforesaid.

A familiar source of conflict is referred to when the instruction finishes: 'And whatever expense should be laid out and expended by him in respect thereof shall be reimbursed by the Corporation (in case the Government should not pay and be at the expense of the same)'.[18]

The threatened invasion never came, since the situation was now changed in France. Hoche, with his hatred of Britain was dead, and the pressure from Wolfe Tone to invade was no longer effective. He would, in any case, soon be dead. Tone met Napoleon, and was not impressed. The fact was though that Napoleon was in command, and in recognising the power of Britain, he realised that because of the British domination of the sea it would be best to attack her in other places. The assault on Pembrokeshire was, famously, the last invasion of Britain.

Notes

Introduction

1   *Cambrian Register 1795*, p.260.
2   *Hassall on Pembrokeshire*, p.61.
3   Roberts, Dafydd, Nhw dedd y chwarelwyr-arwyr y fro, *The Pembrokeshire slate quarrymen Llafur* No.5 No.1. No date.
4   Phillips ,J.R., *The history of Cilgerran*, p.p159–164.
5   *Cambrian Register 1795*, pp.254—5
6   Wigstead, *Remarks on a tour etc.* p62.
7   Hoare, *Journals of tours in Wales* section 24 p.490.
8   Edwards, George, *The coal industry in Pembrokeshire* p.1.
9   *Hassall on Pembrokeshire* p.18.
10 Davies, Walter(Gwallter Mechain), *General view of the agriculture and domestic economy of south Wales etc.* pp.187–188.
11 Jones, Francis, *The Vaughans of Golden Grove IV,* Tory Coed-Shenfield-Golden Grove, THSC, 1966, p.159.
12 Report of the Commissioners of Inquiry into the state of education in Wales, appointed by the Committee of Council on education 1847, Part 1, known as, and hereafter referred to as 'The Blue Books', the colloquial and abusive term. P.422.
13 Fenton, *A historical tour through Pembrokeshire* p.8.
14 Laws, *The history of Little England beyond Wales* p.367.
15 Walker, Margaret S., *The Reverend Henry Vincent* p.70.
16 Williams, Gwyn A., 'Beginnings of radicalism', in *The remaking of Wales in the eighteenth century.* p.126.
17 Salmon, *The French invasion of Pembrokeshire in 1797* p.198
18 Fenton op. cit. p.9.
19 Jones, E.H. Stuar,t *The last invasion of Britain* p.211
20 Rose, *The French at Fishguard* p.84

Chapter 1
The People of Pembrokeshire in 1797

1   Howell, D.W., *The rural poor* p.102

2   ibid. p.107.

3   ibid. p.112.

4   Charles, B.G., *The Place-Names of Pembrokeshire*, under Ffynnon: and Baker Jones, D.L,
      Ffynone, Pembrokeshire, p.116.

5   Thomas, Peter D.G., *Politics in eighteenth century Wales* p.8.

6   G.E.C., *Complete Baronetcy, Creations by James I*, under Philips.

7   Or as has been insisted, Stackpool, by Nicholas, *Annals and antiquities of the counties
      and county families of Wales* p.897.

8   Thomas, Peter D.G., op. cit. p.8

9   *Hassall on Pembrokeshire* p.13

10   Duffy, M., *The Younger Pitt* p.41

11   Fenton, op. cit., pp.131–2

12   NLW 1352Bff.310–14, quoted Howells B.E. and K.A., *Pembrokeshire Life*.

13   Jones, Stuart, op. cit. p.10

14   Howells B.E. and K.A., *Pembrokeshire Life*, 112–114, quoted Roland Thorne and
      Robert Howell, *Pembrokeshire in Wartime 1793–1815* p.380.

15   Fenton quoted by Francis Jones, *Historic houses of Pembrokeshire and their families*, under
      Llanion.

16   Fenton, op. cit. p.259

17   Gwinfardd Dyfed, in *Cambrian Register 1795*, p.261

18   Baker-Jones, D.L., *Ffynone, Pembrokeshire*, p.118. See also Jones, *Historic Houses*, under
      Ffynnone.

19   Owen, Bryn, *History of the Welsh Militia and Volunteer Corps 1757-1908*:
      Carmarthenshire, Pembrokeshire & Cardiganshire (Part 1) pp.75–6. See also Baker-
      Jones D.L., *Ffynone, Pembrokeshire* pp.129–36, where he rehearses the claim that he
      misappropriated his nephew's money.

20   Jones, Stuart, op. cit. p.255

21   Howell, *Patriarchs and parasites*, p.173

22   ibid.

23   ibid. p.181

24   ibid.

25   ibid. p.182

26   Malkin, The *scenery, antiquities and biography of South Wales*, p.430.

27   Howell, *Patriarchs and Parasites* p.80

28   *Blue Books on Education*, Part 1, p.401

29   ibid. p.226

30   ibid p.229

31   PRO HO 42/35.

32   Pembrokeshire RO, D/Lewis/1/83.

33   Fenton, op. cit. p.306.

34   Howell, David W., *The economy of the landed estates of Pembrokeshire c. 1680-1830*, WHR
      3 1966-7, pp.269ff

35   ibid. p.275.

36   ibid p.270

37 Davies, Walter Volume 1 p.123
38 Quoted in Twiston Davies and Edwards, *Welsh life in the eighteenth century*, p.17
39 ibid. p.19.
40 Malloy, *And they blessed Rebecca*, p.247.
41 ibid. p.16, quoting *The Times*, 7 October 1843.
42 *Hassall on Pembrokeshire* p.57
43 Blue Books, part 1 p.401
44 ibid. p.447.
45 Phillips, J.B, *The history of Cilgerran*, p.11
46 Royal Commission on Land in Wales and Monmouthshire, 1986, Volume 11, p.567.
47 Barber, J.T., *A tour through Wales and Monmouthshire*, pp.56–8
48 Evans, J., *Letters written during a tour through South Wales*, p.278
49 Blue Books Part 1 p.9
50 *Carmarthenshire Antiquarian Society and Field Club Transactions vol. xxiv 1939* pp.24–5
51 Mayor of Pembroke to Newcastle June 17 1740, and William Owen to Newcastle SP Domestic 36/50/51: quoted D.G. Isaac's *A study of popular disturbances in Britain 1714-1795*, pp.34–35, and Ashton, T.S., and Sykes, J., *The coal industry of the eighteen century*, p.119.
52 Thorne and Powell, *Pembrokeshire in wartime, 1793-1815*, p.379.
53 PRO HO 42/35.
54 Knox, Some account of the Proceedings etc., p.90.
55 PRO HO 42/61.
56 Quoted Bullen, *Milford Marathon*, p.7.
57 ibid. p.13
58 NLW MS 1352 B. ff. 357-60, quoted Howells, B.E., and Howells, K.A., *Pembrokeshire Life 1572 -1843*, pp.86–7.
59 PRO HO 42/34
60 Jones, Stuart, p.254
61 Salmon, *The French invasion of Pembrokeshire*, p.158.
62 Gwinfardd Dyfed, p.256
63 Evans, J., Letters written etc. p.305.
64 Gwinfardd Dyfed, p.240.
65 ibid., p.260.
66 ibid. p.254–5.
67 Fenton, op. cit. pp.72–3.
68 Saunders, Erasmus, The state of education etc. p.14.
69 *Welsh Political and Educational Leaders in the Victorian Era* ed. Morgan, J.Vyrnwy, *Entry on the Right Reverend William Basil Jones* by Canon Gregory Smith p.150.
70 Salmon, *The French invasion of Pembrokeshire*, p.137

Chapter 2
France, the Revolution, and the Invasion

1 Davies, Hywel; *Morgan John Rhys and James Bicheno*, p.111
2 ibid. p.120
3 ibid. p.122

4   Williams, Gwyn A., *The beginnings of radicalism*, p.112.
5   Evans, Geraint, *Foundations of Modern Wales*, p.210
6   ibid. p.209
7   Williams, Glanmor; Jones, Griffith, in *The International Biography of Adult Education*.
8   Spurrell, William, *Carmarthen and its neighbourhood*, p.120
9   Davies, David, *The influence of the French Revolution*, p.207.
10   Thomas, D.O., *Richard Price and America*, p.41.
11   Davies, David, op. cit. p.209.
12   PRO HO 42/24.
13   Davies, David, op. cit. p.18.
14   ibid. pp.179–184.
15   Williams, David, *The mission of David Williams and James Tilley Matthews to England 1793*.
16   Thomas, D.O., *Response to Revolution*, p.61–3
17   Davies, David op. cit. p.60–1
18   This point is frequently stressed by David Davies, passim.
19   Davies, David op. cit. pp.24–26
20   Davies, Hywel, *Morgan John Rhys and James Bicheno*, p124.
21   Williams, Gwyn A., *Beginnings of Radicalism*, pp.133–4.
22   Davies, David, op. cit. p.43
23   Williams, Gwyn A.; *Morgan John Rhees and his Beulah* pp.442–3
24   Twiston Davies and Edwards, op. cit. pp.143–4.
25   Davies, David, op. cit. p.147
26   ibid. p.156.
27   ibid. p.155.
28   ibid. p.156
29   ibid. p.93
30   ibid. pp.195–6.
31   ibid. p.198.
32   ibid. p.31.
33   Twiston Davies and Edwards, op. cit. p.vii.
34   Colyer, Richard J., *The Welsh cattle drovers*, p.45.
35   Wager, D., *Welsh politics and parliamentary reform*, p.431.
36   Williams, Gwyn A., *Beginnings of radicalism*, p.117.
37   Williams, Gwyn A., *Locating a Welsh working class*, p.27.
38   ibid. p.18–19.
39   Fenton op. cit. p.10
40   Twiston Davies and Edwards, op.cit. p.40
41   Forrest, Alan, *The French Revolution*, p.121
42   Lyons, Martyn, *France under the Directory*, p.191.
43   Forrest, op. cit. p.125
44   Lyons, op. cit. p.54
45   Elliott, Marianne, *Wolfe Tone: Prophet of Irish independence*, p.355
46   ibid. p.298
47   Elliot's title, supra.
48   ibid. p.281
49   ibid. p.306.
50   See Stuart Jones pp.17ff for details.
51   Gill, C., *The naval mutinies of 1797*, p.330

52 ibid. p.330.
53 ibid. pp.331–2.
54 ibid. pp.337–8.
55 Lyons, op. cit. p.192.
56 Elliott, op. cit. p.297.
57 ibid.p.332.
58 ibid.
59 Salmon, *The French invasion*, p.133.
60 ibid. pp.134–5, (his italics).
61 Williams, A.L., op. cit., p.8.
62 Jones, Stuart, op. cit. p.47. Monroe was the Fifth President of the United States, elected in 1816, and in 1820.
63 ibid. p.50.
64 Turner, F.J., *The policy of France towards the Mississippi Valley in the period of Washington and Adams*, p.262.
65 Jones, Stuart, op. cit. p.53.
66 Rutland, *Journal*, p.133.
67 Jones, Stuart, op. cit. p.276.
68 ibid. p.277
69 Kinross, John, *Fishguard Fiasco*, p.116.
70 Jones, Stuart, op. cit.p.250.
71 Cwmgwili Manuscripts Carmarthen Antiquarian Society Transactions Part LXVII quoted Stuart Jones, p.124.
72 Transactions of the Carmarthenshire Antiquarian Society, VIII, 79, quoted Salmon, *The French invasion*, p.197
73 Rose, Richard, *The French at Fishguard*, p.77 and his Appendix, p.102.
74 Jones, Stuart, op. cit. p.54.
75 Desbrière, E., *Projets et tentative de debarquement aux Isles Britanniques*, translated Wheeler and Broadley *Napoleon and the invasion of England* Volume 1 p.239. See also Salmon, *The French invasion of Britain*, p.135
76 PRO Bouillon Correspondence WO 1/9
77 Carmarthenshire RO, Cawdor Papers 223, quoted Richard Rose, op. cit., p.76
78 ibid.
79 Rose, op. cit. p.76
80 Salmon, *The French invasion*, pp.135–6.
81 ibid. pp.136–9.
82 Salmon, *The French invasion*, pp.135–139

Chapter 3
The Invasion

1 Elliott, op. cit., p.333.
2 PRO HO 42/40 quoted Stuart Jones op. cit. p.154.
3 Salmon, *The French invasion*, p.139.
4 ibid. p.142–3.
5 ibid. p.143–4.

6   As always with Welsh place names, there are wide variations in print. These are examples: A.L. Williams writes Carrig Gwasted, John Harries goes for Cerrig Gwastad, while the present Ordnance Survey spelling is Carregwastad. The two words in Welsh which form the name are Carreg (Rock) and Gwastad (level or flat), with the appropriate mutation.

7   Rose op. cit. p.78.

8   Williams, A.L., op. cit. p.6.

9   ibid. p.7

10 Salmon, *The French invasion*, pp. 141–2.

11 For a full account see Stuart Jones, op. cit., Appendix IV

12 Fenton, op. cit. p.8.

13 op. cit pp. 106–7

14 Williams, A.L., op. cit. p.31.

15 Walter, *Truthful history of the last invasion of Britain*, pp. 25–6.

16 Salmon, *The French invasion*, p. 138.

17 Williams, A.L., p.23

18 PRO HO 42/40, quoted Salmon, op. cit. pp. 168–9.

19 ibid. p. 169.

20 ibid. p. 170.

21 Jones, F., *Harries of Tregwynt*, p. 117.

22 For example, Stuart Jones op. cit. p.89.

23 ibid. p.92

24 Bullen, *Milford Marathon*, p.2

25 ibid. p.9.

26 ibid. p.12.

27 ibid.

28 Glover, Michael, *That astonishing infantry*, p.36.

29 Western, J.R., *The English militia in the eighteenth century*, p.269.

30 Howell, *The Rural Poor*, pp. 203–5.

31 ibid. p.204.

32 PRO HO 42/52.

33 Western op. cit. pp. 418–9.

34 Western, J.R., *The Volunteer Movement as an anti revolutionary force*, p.607

35 ibid. p.606.

36 ibid. p.613.

37 ibid. p.610.

38 ibid. p.609.

39 Owen, Bryn, *History of the Welsh Militia and Volunteer Corps*, p.98.

40 Fellows and Freeman, *Historical Records* etc., p.2

41 ibid. p.325.

42 Gore, John, *The last invasion of Britain*, p.271.

43 Jones, *Vaughans of Golden Grove*, IV, p.179.

44 ibid. p.180.

45 Salmon, *The French invasion*, pp. 156–7.

46 Owen, Bryn, op. cit. p.98.

47 Carmarthenshire RO, Cawdor, 223/16.

48 Knox, Thomas, *Some account of the proceedings that took place on the landing of the French near Fishguard on the 22nd February 1797* etc. p.4.

49 Tableau D'organisation de la 2e Legions des Francs, in Carmarthenshire RO, Cawdor 223, Rose p.76.

50 Dale-Jones, *Arrivals and departures*, p.107, quoting Carmarthenshire RO Cawdor 223
51 Salmon, *The French invasion*, p.167.
52 Knox, op. cit. p.44.
53 Jones, Stuart, op. cit. p.101.
54 Fenton, op. cit. p.9.
55 Walker, *The Reverend Henry Vincent*, p.7.
56 Jones, Stuart, op. cit. p.102.
57 Fenton op. cit. p.72
58 ibid.
59 H.L. Williams, p.10
60 ibid.
61 Warburton, *The History of Solva*, p.25.
62 Jones, Stuart, op. cit. p.103–4
63 Rutland, op. cit. p.127–8
64 Jones, Stuart, op. cit. p.104
65 Rutland, op. cit. p.128
66 Harries, John, *Welsh patriotism*, p.17.
67 Quoted Dale-Jones, p.112.
68 Laws, *The history of little England beyond Wales*, p.368.
69 Jones, Stuart, op. cit. p.105.
70 Kinross, *Fishguard fiasco*, p.58.
71 Jones, Stuart, op. cit. p.105.
72 Rutland, op. cit. p.132.
73 Kinross, op. cit. p.58.
74 Jones, Stuart, op. cit. p.105.
75 Carradice, *The last invasion*, p.83.
76 Williams, H.L., op. cit. p.16.
77 Salmon, *The French invasion*, p.170.
78 ibid.
79 Rutland, op. cit. p.132.
80 Dale-Jones, op. cit. p.111.
81 Stuart Jones, op. cit. p.106.
82 Harries, John, op. cit. p.8
83 Rutland, op. cit. p.136.
84 ibid. p.136–7.
85 Williams, H.L., op. cit. p.17.
86 Carmarthenshire RO, Cawdor 223/8/1.
87 Stuart Jones discusses exactly when, op. cit. p.257.
88 Both letters were published in the Annual Register, 1797.
89 Williams, H.L., op. cit. p.18
90 Rutland, op. cit. p.138.
91 ibid.
92 Salmon, *The French invasion*, p.167.
93 Rutland, p.139.
94 Dale-Jones, op. cit. p.109.
95 ibid.
96 ibid. p.109.
97 PRO HO 42/40.
98 Cawdor; letter to his wife: The assumption is that he escorted Morrison, not Norris. Salmon, *The French invasion*, p.165.

99   Jones, Stuart, op. cit. pp.250–1, gives a detailed biography.

100 Salmon, *The French invasion*, p.146.

101 These depositions are PRO PC 1/37 A114 and are reproduced in Horn Pamela. *The last invasion of Britain*, pp.19–22.

102 Salmon, *The French invasion*, p.152.

103 ibid. Cawdor, letter to his wife.

104 Harries, op. cit. p.20.

105 Davies, David, op. cit. p.229

106 Salmon, *The French invasion*, p.158.

107 ibid. p.152

108 Abell, Francis, *Prisoners of War in Britain*, p.41.

109 Howard, John, *The State of the Prisons*, p.465.

110 ibid. p.456.

111 ibid.

112 Rutland, op. cit. pp.161–2.

113 Howard, op. cit. pp.188–9.

114 ibid. p.189.

115 ibid.

116 Salmon, *The French invasion*, p.152.

117 Rutland op. cit. p.141.

118 Quoted Walters op. cit., p.102. Flux is dysentery, or variants of it.

119 Williams, A.I., op. cit. pp.26ff.

120 Laws op. cit. p.374.

121 Esquirol, Anne-Marie, *Pierre-Honoré Boudon de Saint Amans*, p.186.

122 James, Douglas, *The history of Haverfordwest Grammar School*, p.14.

123 Labit, Anne-Marie, op. cit. p.9

124 Abell, op. cit. p.365.

125 Labit, Anne-Marie, op. cit. p.9

126 ibid. p.10.

127 Kinross, op. cit. p.91.

128 Esquirol, Anne-Marie, op. cit. p.187

129 Rutland, op. cit. pp.140–144.

130 ibid. p.141.

131 Salmon, *The French invasion*, p.168.

132 Rutland, op. cit. pp.142–3

133 ibid. p.141.

134 Rose op. cit. p.92, quoting PRO ADM 102/283.

135 ibid., pp.91–2.

136 Salmon, *The French invasion*, p.159.

137 Stuart Jones, p.125.

138 McConville, Sean, *A history of prison administration*, p.107.

139 Abell, op. cit. p.41.

140 ibid. p.93

141 Rutland, op. cit. p.184.

142 Rose, op. cit. p.82, quoting Carmarthenshire RO Cawdor 223/8/1.

143 Harries op. cit. pp.11–12.

144 Stuart Jones, op. cit. p.141.

145 Salmon, *The French invasion*, p.170.

146 Rose, op. cit. p.79 quoting N.L.W. *Great Sessions* 4 Wales 826–5 (No.42 in bundle).

147 Fellows and Freeman, op. cit. p.325

148 See Stuart Jones, op. cit. Appendix V, for a detailed history of the regiment.

Chapter 4
The Aftermath: Cowardice and Treason?

1 Howell, *Patriarchs and Parasites*, p.136.

2 Jones, Geraint, *The foundations of modern Wales*, p.307.

3 ibid. p.306

4 Gwinfardd Dyfed, *Cambrian Register*, p.261

5 Jones, Stuart, op. cit. p.86.

6 PRO HO 43/37.

7 Gwinfardd Dyfed, on Knox, op. cit.

8 Knox, Some account etc., Appendix.

9 Salmon, *The French invasion*, p.177.

10 *Chambers Biographical Dictionary*, under 'Picton'.

11 Davies, Walter, *General view of the agriculture* etc., Volume 1, p.368.

12 The entire letter can be found in Salmon, op. cit. p.177.

13 ibid. p.181.

14 Salmon, *The French invasion*, p.178.

15 ibid.

16 Jones, Stuart, op. cit. p.188.

17 Salmon, *The French invasion*, p.178.

18 ibid. p.179.

19 ibid. p.180.

20 Salmon, D., *Cymmrodor*, vol.XLIII, quoted Jones, p.193.

21 Salmon, *The French invasion*, pp.182–3.

22 Jones, Stuart, op. cit. p.263.

23 Salmon, *The French invasion*, p.184.

24 Jones, Stuart, op. cit. pp.183–4.

25 Knox, op. cit. p.90

26 Jones, Stuart, op. cit. p.187.

27 Knox op. cit. pp.75–6.

28 ibid. pp.81–2.

29 PRO HO 50/6, quoted Jones, p.201–2.

30 PRO HO50/40, quoted Jones, p.202.

31 Walters, op. cit. pp.54–5.

32 Jones, Stuart, op. cit. p.103.

33 Walters, op. cit. p.25 and p.27.

34 ibid.

35 Stackpole Letters, transcribed by Edward Laws, NLW 1352b, quoted Stuart Jones, pp.193–4.

36 ibid. p.203.

37 ibid. p.265.

38 ibid. p.211.

39 ibid. p.212.

40   Walter, op, cit. p.102
41   Jones, Stuart, op. cit. p.212
42   PRO Wales, 28/190, quoted Stuart Jones, p.236.
43   Jones, Stuart, op. cit. p.240.
44   *The Times*, 18 September 1797.
45   These are printed in David Salmon, 'A sequel to the French invasion of
     Pembrokeshire', in *Y Cymmrodor, The magazine of the Honourable Society of
     Cymmrodorion*, vol.xliii, 1932.
46   Jones, Stuart, op. cit. p.223
47   *The Times*, supra.
48   Rutland, op. cit. pp.161–2.
49   Quoted Walters, op. cit. p.103.
50   The whole episode is described in Rutland, pp.159–60.
51   ibid. p.137.
52   Fenton, op. cit. p.10.
53   PRO HO 43/4
54   PRO HO 30/8
55   Jones, Stuart, op. cit. p.244.
56   ibid. p.231.
57   Jones, Stuart, op. cit. p.222.
58   ibid. p.223.
59   Fenton, op. cit. p.10.

Chapter 5
The Creation of Myths and Legends

1   Salmon, *The French invasion*, p.163
2   Pembrokeshire RO HAD/838/6.
3   Printed in *The Pembrokeshire Historian*, No.3, 1971.
4   Salmon, *The French invasion*, p.161.
5   Parish Register, Roch, Pembrokeshire RO, HPR/32/1.
6   Harries, op. cit. pp.11–12
7   This is from PRO HO 50/242. Letter from Jonathan Lovett to the duke of Portland
     quoted Roland Quinault *The French invasion of Pembrokeshire in 1797*, p.619.
8   Salmon, *The French invasion*, p.156.
9   Sarah Farley's *Bristol Journal* 4 March 1797.
10   Quinault, *The French invasion of Fishguard*, p.630.
11   Jones, Stuart, op. cit. p.102.
12   Harries, op. cit. p.11.
13   ibid. p.10.
14   Williams, H.L., op. cit. p.24.
15   Jones, Stuart, op. cit. pp.212–215.
16   Salmon, *The French invasion*, p.146.
17   ibid. p.151.
18   ibid. pp.161–2.
19   ibid. p.165.

20 Jones, Stuart, op. cit. pp.285–6.
21 Rutland, op. cit. p.127.
22 Tone, W.T.W, *Life of Wolfe Tone*, p.153.
23 Rutland, op. cit. p.133.
24 Salmon, *The French invasion*, p.145.
25 Rutland, op. cit. p.145.
26 Kinross, op. cit. p.63.
27 Rutland, op. cit. p.161.
28 ibid. p.127.
29 ibid. p.129.
30 ibid. p.183.
31 ibid. pp.186–7.
32 ibid. p.130.
33 ibid. p.137.
34 ibid. p.161
35 Walters op. cit. p.101.
36 Gore, John, *The last invasion of Britain*, p.270.
37 Rutland, op. cit. p.131.
38 Salmon, *The French invasion*, p.162.
39 Harries, op. cit. p.6.
40 Jones, Stuart, op. cit. p.72
41 ibid. p.83.
42 Williams, H.L., op. cit. pp.32–3.
43 ibid. p.13.
44 Rose, op. cit. p.79.
45 Jones, Stuart, op. cit. p.123.
46 Laws, op. cit. p.372.
47 Williams, H.L., op. cit. pp.29–30.
48 Laws, op. cit. p.372.
49 Williams, H.L., op. cit. p.30
50 Salmon, *The French invasion*, p.160.
51 Gore, John, op. cit. *The Quarterly Review.*
52 Salmon, *The French invasion*, p.156.
53 Williams, H.L. p.21.
54 NLW Ms 13209D, Rose, op. cit. p.98.
55 ibid. p.101.
56 Williams, H.L., op. cit. p.22
57 Ferrar Fenton quoted Stuart Jones, op. cit. p.118.
58 See, for example, Gore, John, op. cit. p.271
59 Davies, David, op. cit p.228.
60 Jones, Stuart, op. cit p.116.
61 ibid. p.117.
62 Williams, H.L., op. cit. p.42.
63 Esquirol, Anne-Marie, op. cit. p.186.
65 Rutland, op. cit. p.184.
66 Salmon, *The French invasion*, p.194.
67 Walker, *The Reverend Henry Vincent*, p.71.
68 Pembrokeshire RO, Q12/214.
69 George, Earl Lloyd, *Lloyd George*, p.18.

70   Bruce, Evangeline, *Napoleon and Josephine*, p.18.
71   Beloff, *Public order and popular disturbances*, p.64
72   ibid. p.68
73   John, Anglea V., *A miner struggle?*, p.72.
74   Howells B.E. and K.A., *Pembrokeshire Life*, p.15.
75   Jones, D.J.V., *Before Rebecca*, p.34.
76   Jones, D.J.V., *Distress and discontent in Cardiganshire*, p.284.
77   Michelet, *History of the French Revolution*, p.288.
78   ibid. p.302.
79   Price, Holland, *The horrors of invasion*.
80   Salmon, *The French invasion*, Letter from Cawdor to his wife, p.166.
81   Quinault, op. cit. p.629.
82   See Williams, H.L., op. cit. p.33
83   Kinross, op. cit. p.58.
84   Davies, David, op. cit. p.228.
85   Jones, Stuart, op. cit. p.105.
86   Walker, op. cit. p.71.
87   Rose, op. cit., p.89.
88   Carradice, op. cit. p.83.
89   Walker, op. cit. p.70.

Epilogue

1   PRO HO 42/40, quoted Horn, op. cit. pp.13–14.
2   PRO PC 1/37.
3   Jones, Stuart, op. cit. pp.137–9. See also his Appendix 11.
4   Salmon, *The French invasion*, p.161.
5   Evans, J., *Letters written during a tour* etc. p.267.
6   Williams, H.L., op. cit. p.36.
7   Dale-Jones, op. cit. pp.109–10.
8   Jones, Stuart, op. cit. p.261.
9   Dale-Jones, op. cit. p.110.
10   Williams, H.L. op. cit. p.35.
11   Jones, Stuart, op. cit. p.151. Jones goes into detail about the ships' movements.
12   Salmon, *The French invasion*, pp.195–6.
13   Clapham, *A history of the bank of England*, pp.271–2.
14   Jones, Stuart, op. cit. p.164.
15   Salmon, *The French invasion*, pp.201–2.
16   ibid. p.201.
17   ibid. p.203.
18   ibid. p.153.

Bibliography

Original Records:

The National Archives, (Public Record Office) (PRO).
The National Library of Wales, Aberystwyth (NLW).
Pembrokeshire Record Office (Pembrokeshire RO).
Pembrokeshire County Library.
Carmarthenshire Record Office (Carmarthenshire RO).
Cwmgwili Manuscripts, Carmarthen Antiquarian Society Transactions Part LXVII.

Official Reports:

Reports of the Commissioners of Enquiry into the state of education in Wales, appointed by the Committee of Council on education 1847: Part 1 Carmarthen, Glamorgan, and Pembroke.
Royal Commission on Land in Wales and Monmouthshire, 1896.

Books:

Abell, Francis, *Prisoners of war in Britain 1758 to 1815: a record of their lives, their romance and their suffering.* (Humphrey Milford, OUP, 1914).
Ap Gwilym, H.L. (Williams, H.L.), *An authentic account of the invasion by the French troops on Cerrig Gwastad Point, near Fishguard, on Wednesday, 22nd February 1797, and their surrender to the forces of His Britannic Majesty on Goodwick Sands on Friday 24th February: likewise some occurrences connected therewith never before published.* (Haverfordwest 1842, second edition 1853.) In the first edition the author signs himself H.L. Ap Gwilym.
Ashton, T.S.; and Sykes, J., *The coal industry of the eighteen century*, (MUP, 1964).

Barber, J.T., *A tour throughout south Wales and Monmouthshire*, (London, 1803).

Beloff, M., *Public order and popular disturbances 1660–1714*, (OUP, 1938).

Bruce, Evangeline, *Napoleon and Josephine: an improbable marriage*, (Weidenfeld and Nicolson, 1995).

Bullen, Mark, *Milford Marathon: the story of the Customs Officers who helped to repel the French invasion of Pembrokeshire in 1797*. (No Publisher listed, 1997).

Carradice, Phil, *The last invasion: the story of the French landing in Wales*, (Village Publishing, Pontypool, 1992.)

Charles, B.G., *The place names of Pembrokeshire*, 2 Volumes, (The National Library of Wales, 1992).

Clapham, Sir John, *The Bank of England 1694–1797: a history*. (CUP, 1944).

Colyer, Richard J., *The Welsh cattle drovers; agriculture and the Welsh cattle trade before and during the nineteenth century*, (UWP, 1976).

Davies, David, *The influence of the French Revolution on Welsh life and literature*, (Carmarthen, 1926).

Davies, Leonard Twiston and Edwards, Averyl, *Welsh life in the eighteenth century*, (London, Country Life, 1939).

Davies, Walter, (Gwallter Mechain), *General view of the agriculture and domestic economy of south Wales; containing the counties of Brecon, Caermarthen, Cardigan, Glamorgan, Pembroke, Radnor*. (London, McMillan, 1814).

Duffy, M., *The younger Pitt*, (Longman, 2000).

Edwards, George, 'The coal industry in Pembrokeshire', *Field Studies* Volume.1, No.5, (1963).

Elliott, Marianne, *Wolfe Tone, Prophet of Irish Independence*, (Yale UP, 1989).

Evans, J., *Letters written during a tour through south Wales in the year 1803 and at other times*, (London, 1804).

Fellows, G., and Freeman, B., *Historical Records of the South Nottinghamshire Hussars Yeomanry 1794–1924*, (Aldershot, printed by Gale and Polden Ltd, 1928).

Fenton, Ferrar, *Landing of the French at Fishguard in 1797, Pembrokeshire Antiquities*, (Solva, 1897).

Fenton, Richard, *A historical tour through Pembrokeshire*. (First published 1811 and republished by Davies and Co. Brecknock, 1903).

Forrest, Alan, *The French Revolution*, (Blackwell, 1995).

G.E.C. (ed.) *Complete baronetage*, Volume 11, 1625–1649, (Exeter Pollard, 1904).

Gill, C., The naval mutinies of 1797, (MUP, 1918).

Glover, Michael, *That astonishing infantry: three hundred years of the history of the Royal Welch Fusiliers (23rd Regiment of Foot) 1689–1989*, (Leo Cooper, 1989).

Harries, John, *Welsh patriotism: or, The landing of the French at Fishguard on the 22nd of February 1797, compiled from authentic sources*. (John Harries, 1875).

Hassall, Charles, *General view of the agriculture of the county of Pembroke with observations on the means of its improvement drawn up for the consideration of the board of agriculture and internal improvement*, (London, 1794). This is noted in the text as 'Hassall on Pembrokeshire'.

Hoare, Sir Richard Colt, *Journals of tours in Wales*, (1796).

Horn, Pamela, *The last invasion of Britain, Fishguard 1797*. (Preseli Printers, 1980).

Howard, John, *The state of the prisons in England and Wales* etc. (London, 1777 and 1792).

Howells, B.E. and K.A., *Pembrokeshire life 1572–1843*, (Pembrokeshire Record Society, 1972).

Howell, David W., *The rural poor in eighteenth century Wales*, (UWP, 2000).

Howell, David W., *Patriarchs and Parasites: the gentry of south-west Wales in the eighteenth century*, (UWP, 1986).

James, Douglas G., *The history of the Haverfordwest Grammar School*, (J.W. Hammond, 1961).

Jenkins, Geraint, *The foundations of modern Wales 1642–1780*, (UWP, 1987).

Jones, David J.V., *Before Rebecca: popular protests in Wales 1793–1835*, (Allen Lane, 1972).

Jones, Stuart E.H., *The last invasion of Britain*, (UWP, 1950).

Jones, Francis, *Historic houses of Pembrokeshire and their families*, (Brawdy Books, Pembrokeshire, 1996).

Kinross, John, *Fishguard Fiasco: An account of the last invasion of Britain* (H.G. Walters, Tenby, 1974).

Knox, Thomas, Some account of the proceedings that took place on the landing of the French near Fishguard on the 22nd February 1797: and of the inquiry held afterwards into Lieut. Col. Knox's conduct on that occasion by order of His Royal Highness the Commander in Chief, together with the official correspondence and other documents London 1800.

Labit, Anne-Marie, *Preface*, (Exposition Saint-Amans Musee d'Agen, 1968).

Laws, Edward, *The history of Little England beyond Wales and the non-kymric colony settled in Pembrokeshire*, (London, 1888).

Lloyd, George Earl, *Lloyd George*, (Frederick Muller, 1960).

Lyons, Martyn, *France under the Directory*, (CUP, 1975).

Malloy, Pat, *And they blessed Rebecca*, (Gomer Press, 1983).

Malkin, B.H., *The scenery, antiquities and biography of south Wales*, (London, 1804, reprinted SR Publishers, 1970).

McConville, Sean, *A history of English prison administration*, Volume 1 1750–1877, (Routledge and Kegan Paul, 1981).

Michelet, Jules, *History of the French Revolution*. Translated by Charles Cocks, edited and with an introduction by Gordon Wright, (Chicago, 1967).

Morgan, J. Vyrnwy (ed.), *Welsh Political and Educational Leaders in the Victorian era. Entry on the Right Reverend William Basil Jones* by Canon Gregory Smith, (Nisbet, London, 1908).

Nicholas, Thomas, *Annals and antiquities of the counties and county families of Wales*, (Genealogical Publishing Company, 1872 and 1875).

Owen, B., *History of the Welsh Militia and Volunteer Corps 1757–1908: Carmarthenshire, Pembrokeshire & Cardiganshire* (Part 1) (Bridge Books, Wrexham, 1995).

Price, Robert Holland, *The horrors of invasion*, (Wrexham, second edition, 1804).

Rutland, John Duke of, *Journal of a tour through North and South Wales and the Isle of Man*, (London, 1805).

Salmon, David, 'The French invasion of Fishguard in 1797. Official documents, contemporary letters, and early narratives', in *West Wales Historical Records* vol. XIV, (W Spurrell and son, 1929).

Saunders, Erasmus, *View of the state of Education in the diocese of St. David's*, (London, 1721).

Spurrell William Carmarthen and its neighbourhood 1879 reprinted 1995 by Dyfed County Council.

Thomas, D.O., *Richard Price and America*, (Aberystwyth, 1975).

Thomas, D.O. *Response to Revolution: how the opening events of the French Revolution were perceived by some prominent Welshmen*. (UWP, 1989).

Thomas, D.O. (ed.), *The correspondence of Richard Price*, (UWP, 1991).

Thorne, R. and Powell, R., 'Pembrokeshire in Wartime. 1793–1815', in *Pembrokeshire County History* Volume III, ed. Brian Howells, (The Pembrokeshire Historical Society, 1987).

Tone, W.T.H., (ed.), *Life and adventures of Theobald Wolfe Tone*, (Burns, Oates and Washbourne, London, 1826).

Walters, Syd, *Truthful history of the last invasion of Britain*, (Newark Editions, Sutton Coldfield, 1989).

Warburton, F.W., *The history of Solva*, (The Blackheath Press, 1944).

Warner, Reverend Richard, *A walk through Wales, in August 1797*. (Cruttwell, London 1798).

Western, J.R., *The English militia in the eighteenth century: the story of a political issue 1660–1902*. (Routledge and Kegan Paul, London, 1965).

Wheeler, H.F.B. and Broadley, A.M., *Napoleon and the invasion of England: the story of the Great Terror*, 2 volumes, (John Lane, 1908).

Wigstead, H., *Remarks on a tour to north and south Wales in the year 1797*, (London, 1800).

Williams, David, 'Wales and the French Revolution', in Roderick, A.J. (ed.) *Wales through the ages*, Vol. II, (Llandybie, 1960).

Williams, Glanmor, entry in Griffith Jones, in *The international biography of adult education* eds. Thomas, J.E. and Elsey, B., (Nottingham, 1985).

Williams, H.L. see Ap Gwilym

Williams, Gwyn A., 'Locating a Welsh working class: the frontier years', in Smith, David, (ed.) *A people and a proletariat; essays in the history of Wales 1780–1980* (Pluto Press in association with Llafur, 1980).

Williams, Gwyn A., Beginnings of radicalism in Herbert, T. and Jones, G.E., *The remaking of Wales in the eighteenth century*, (UWP, 1988).

Articles:

Abbreviations

BBCS (Bulletin of the Board of Celtic Studies)
THSC (The Transactions of the Honourable Society of Cymmrodorion)
WHR (Welsh History Review)

Baker-Jones, D.L., 'Ffynone, Pembrokeshire: notes on a country house and its occupants', *THSC* Session 1965, Part I.

Dale-Jones, Edna, 'Arrivals and departures-Carmarthen 1797', *The Carmarthenshire Antiquary* Volume xxxiii (1997).

Davies, Hywel, 'Morgan John Rhys and James Bicheno: Anti-Christ and the French Revolution in England and Wales', *BBCS* Volume XXIX Part I (November 1980).

Esquirol, Anne-Marie, 'Pierre-Honoré Boudon de Saint Amans (1774–1858) et Angleterre', *Revue de L'Agenais* (April–June 2006).

Gore, John, 'The last invasion of Britain', *The Quarterly Review* (April 1935).

'Gwinfardd Dyfed', 'A statistical account of the parish of Fishguard', *Cambrian Register 1795*, (published 1796).

Howell, David W., 'The economy of the landed estates of Pembrokeshire c.1680-1830', *WHR* (1966–7).

John, Angela V., 'A miner struggle? Women's protests in Welsh Mining history', *Llafur*, Volume 4, No. I, (1984).

Jones, D.J.V., 'Distress and discontent in Carmarthenshire', *Ceredigion* Vol. V No. 3, (1966).

Jones, F., 'Harries of Tregwynt', *THSC*, Sessions 1943 and 1944 (published 1946).

Jones, Francis, 'The Vaughans of Golden Grove IV, Tory Coed-Shenfield-Golden Grove', *THSC*, (1966).

Quinault Roland, 'The French invasion of Fishguard in 1797: a Bicentennial Assessment', *WHR* Vol.19 No.4, (December 1999).

Roberts, 'Dafydd Nhw dedd y chwarelwyr-arwyr y' from 'The Pembrokeshire slate quarrymen', *Llafur* No. 5 No.1, (no date).

Rose, Richard, 'The French at Fishguard; Fact, Fiction and Folklore' *THSC* 2000 New Series Vol.7 (2001).

Salmon, David, 'A sequel to the French invasion of Pembrokeshire', *Y Cymmrodor* Vol.xliii, (1932).

Turner, F.J., 'The policy of France towards the Mississippi Valley in the period of Washington and Adams', *American Historical Review*, Vol. X No.2, (January 1905).

Wager, D., 'Welsh politics and parliamentary reform 1780–1832', *WHR* Vol.7 No.4 (December, 1975).

Walker, Margaret S., 'The Reverend Henry Vincent 1793-1865, a neglected Pembrokeshire Antiquarian', *The Journal of the Pembrokeshire Historical Society*, (1994).

Western, J.R., 'The Volunteer Movement as an Anti-Revolutionary force 1793-1801', *The English Historical Review*, Vol.71, (1956).

Williams, David, 'The mission of David Williams and James Tilley Matthews to England 1793', Vol. LIII *The English Historical Review*, (1938).

Williams, Gwyn A,. 'Morgan John Rhees and his Beulah', *WHR* III (1967).

Dissertation:

Isaac, D.G., 'A study of popular disturbances in Britain 1714-1795', (PhD Edinburgh, 1953).

Index

If you are interested in purchasing other books published by Tempus,
or in case you have difficulty finding any Tempus books in your local bookshop,
you can also place orders directly through our website

www.tempus-publishing.com